Structural Cybernetics: An Overview

Meyer, N. Dean

Key words: organizational structure, organizational design, organizational health, teamwork, reengineering.

N. Dean Meyer and Associates Inc.
641 Danbury Road, Suite D
Ridgefield, CT 06877 USA

203-431-0029

ISBN   0-9641635-1-9

Printed in the United States of America.

THE THEORY

NDMA provided a well-thought-out philosophy of organizational structure, and a practical process for implementing that vision.

> David A. Hall
> Manager, Computing and Information Systems
> Corning Telecommunications Products
> Division

The Structural Cybernetics study is amazingly comprehensive. I was able to find in it answers to just about every question I had throughout our reorganization process.

> Harold Wu
> Director, Systems Branch
> Ontario Ministry of Government Services

Well written, pithy, and easily understood....

> CIO Canada Magazine

THE RESULTS

[Structural Cybernetics is] an organizational theory that positions technology departments to be strategically aligned with their successful, forward-looking companies.

> Judy Shapiro
> Vice President and Director of I.S.
> SmithKline Beecham US Pharmaceuticals

Structural Cybernetics represents a necessary ingredient for I.T.'s survival, success and ultimate acceptance by a corporation as an enabling contributor to the bottom line.

> Harold S. Mawhinney
> Senior Vice President
> The Investors Group

Now, we are well positioned to participate in, and perhaps lead, Sonoco's commitment to total quality management.

> Bernie Campbell
> Vice President, Information Systems
> Sonoco Products Company

Structural Cybernetics... builds an entrepreneurial culture based on customer focus and product orientation, and transforms internal competition into high-performance teamwork.

> Computer Dealer News

THE PROCESS

We are doing something many others are only talking about: reengineering our information services organization. The significant difference between just studying the issues and actually doing it is that NDMA has taken its research beyond conclusions.... It has also provided a process to guide the I.S. executive through implementation. Nowhere else was I able to find that kind of help.

> Mel Hochhalter
> Director, Information Services
> Nike

Structural Cybernetics presents a process by which an organization redesigns itself. The effort is participatory but controlled, and is calculated to yield a technically good solution that has very strong internal support.

> Mark Luker
> Chief Information Officer
> University of Wisconsin at Madison

Meyer's theory certainly isn't glib. His methodology is detailed, right down to the agenda for each meeting....

> Information Week

Once we adopted the [Structural Cybernetics] principles, we had a framework that provided a basis for any decision, defused the inevitable turf battles before they ever began, and accelerated our learning process in a way that probably could not have occurred otherwise.

John Benci
General Director, M.I.S.
The Canadian Wheat Board

The Structural Cybernetics process forced us to specify our products and services, [and] our customers and suppliers for each operating and support organization within our [department]. This brought to light many of the inefficiencies that we had been struggling with and allowed us to deal with them.

William T. Houghton
President
Chevron Information Technology Company

Having the [implementation] process defined and facilitated freed our team to creatively define charters to best serve our clients and coworkers.

Preston Simons
Vice President, Information Systems
Rush Prudential Health Plans

To Bud and Bee Meyer.

CONTENTS

FIGURES

Foreword

Political in-fighting, limited teamwork, lack of customer focus, weak strategic alignment, slow pace of innovation, fragmentation and disintegration, a bureaucratic rather than entrepreneurial culture, pressure for decentralization and outsourcing, poor morale, and too much management time spent resolving internal problems....

Why do these familiar problems seem so ingrained in organizations? Because they are. Many performance problems are unintentionally designed into the organization's structure.

Organizational structure is a science, not a matter of personalities, politics, fads, and intuition. There are twelve fundamental building blocks of structure present in any organization. The way these are combined determines the health and performance of the organization. And the mechanisms of teamwork determine whether or not the organizational design actually works.

Structural Cybernetics is a comprehensive treatment of the issues of organizational design. This brief overview presents the basics of organizational theory, clear definitions of the building blocks of structure, practical principles for designing organization charts, and an approach to high-performance teamwork based on a "network" of entrepreneurs.

Structural Cybernetics
An Overview

PREFACE: The Systematic Executive

The vast majority of us earn a living by working in organizations. Whether they are comprised of a handful or a hundred thousand people, organizations are the primary productive entities in the world. And the effectiveness of an organization impacts people's job satisfaction and lifestyle. Therefore, it is extremely important that we make organizations work very well. In fact, building a healthy organization should be every executive's top priority.

How can an executive improve the health of an organization?

Some approaches are guaranteed to fail. For example, the slash-and-burn mentality of the monomaniacal cost cutter is short sighted. While it delivers short-term savings, it may also damage the effectiveness, especially the flexibility, of the organization. Meanwhile, people are disempowered and morale is severely damaged when carefully engineered business processes are forced on them by efficiency experts.

Building a healthy organization is not a matter of reengineering a few processes, adding a few new functions, or simply preaching the values of quality and customer focus. Executives must do more than fine-tune existing practices, or lead the way on a few high-profile projects. They must fundamentally change the way the organization works, empowering people at every level while guiding them toward individual excellence and high-performance teamwork.

Leaders Versus Managers

To achieve this ambitious goal, the leader's role must change dramatically from past models. Traditionally, executives have been trained to make tough decisions, lead key projects, and manage by wandering around and personally guiding people throughout the organization. These executives quickly became bottlenecks, while wasting much of the talent in their organizations.

Put simply, the model of the executive as a "foreman" is obsolete. In a business environment of rapid change on many fronts, executives cannot afford to work example-at-a-time. If they focus on today's events, they'll be too busy to focus on transformational work (which, it seems, can always be postponed). And they'll be too close to the problems to see the "forest for the trees."

Of course, there are times when an executive must step into the day-to-day operations and fix a severe problem. But an executive can never have enough time to solve every new problem.

Executives must also supervise people, a day-to-day task. "Growing" good people has a tremendous impact. But coaching individuals is painfully slow as a channel for change.

The problem with firefighting and people management is the lack of leverage. Sure, it's fun to make tough decisions and lead the charge on critical projects. But the most effective executives tap all the bright minds in the organization rather than depend solely on the one at the top. By building an organizational environment that sends the right signals, executives can impact a multitude of decisions, as if they were present to gently guide everyone at all times.

The most important job of the executive is to design an organization in which everyone can succeed.

This captures the essence of the word "leadership" -- in contrast to the managerial duties one might also fulfill. The leadership portion of one's job is the time spent improving the way the organization operates. The managerial portion is the time spent supervising people and doing the day-to-day work of the organization.

To have a lasting effect, executives must work at the leadership level on aspects of the organization that do not change too quickly -- not at the management level on the information, materials, and products that the organization processes. For example, the executive who works on a client's strategic problem is delivering a day-to-day product of the organization, not improving the organization's effectiveness. By contrast, the executive who introduces methods for identifying clients' strategic problems enables the whole organization to pursue strategic value day after day.

The *systematic executive* is a leader who works on the underlying processes that guide an organization's day-to-day functioning. This is a higher level than the routine business processes which produce the organization's products and services. The focus of the systematic executive is the *organizational operating system* that guides everyone in every aspect of their work.

The Organizational Operating System

Organizations are like computer systems: they can be programmed to succeed, or they can be filled with bugs.

Let's be perfectly clear about this. *People* cannot be programmed. But executives can design organizations to send the right signals to people. Just as road signs can either clearly direct you or lead you the wrong way, organizations can either guide people toward high-performance teamwork or create choas.

Oddly enough, many executives know how to program a computer (or at least a spreadsheet), but few know how to program their organizations. Yet this is the key to everyone's success.

The science of organizational design is a major part of the science of leadership.

Consider how organizations affect people's performance: Organizations generate a system of influences that guides people so they can work in parallel on interrelated tasks and still produce a common set of products.

By automatically coordinating people, a healthy organization is the key to empowerment. If the organization is designed properly, people can make decisions independently, and the signals throughout the organizational environment will guide people to make the right decisions for the organization as a whole. This is a state of *organizational alignment.*

If an organization can be viewed as a set of parallel, programmable systems, what can an executive control without slipping into the day-to-day activities that lack leverage? There are a number of dimensions of an organization that are "programmed" (consciously or unconsciously) by an executive, including the following:

* **Culture:** the behavioral patterns (habits and conventions) and values generally adopted within the organization.

* **Structure:** the definition of jobs and the reporting hierarchy (organization chart), as well as the processes that combine people into teams as work flows across organizational boundaries.

* **Internal economy:** the budgeting, priority setting, chargeback, and project-approval processes which determine how resources flow through the organization and to its clients.

* **Methods and skills:** the procedures, methodologies, and skills that people in the organization use.

* **Metrics and rewards:** the feedback loops that inform people about how they are doing in time to adjust their behavior, and the incentives for improving performance.

Of these, structure is the most fundamental. Without a healthy structure, cultural principles will be seen as empty exhortations; the internal economy will incite greater friction as entrepreneurs compete for business; methods will not find a home; and metrics will exacerbate unclear and conflicting objectives.

As a means of reprogramming these fundamental organizational forces, structure is an extremely powerful tool that leaders can use to orchestrate significant transformations.

THE LOGIC OF
ORGANIZATIONS

1. The Organizational Crisis

Organizations face much more complex challenges since the broader business environment has grown in complexity.

Any viable business, or a staff "business within a business" such as an Information Systems (I.S.) department, must meet a number of challenging objectives. It must proactively build partnerships with clients, and help them find breakthrough opportunities for its products. It must help clients form consortia to address cross-functional needs. It must help clients defend budgets for the organization's products, and set proper priorities. It must be prepared to satisfy any legitimate (funded) demand, without being constrained by current resources or technologies. It must lead the company with technology innovation across a broad range of product lines. (In I.S., this includes all forms of computing, telecommunications, client-server platforms, management science, library science, artificial intelligence, teleconferencing, etc.) It must collaborate across disciplines in order to build complex multi-disciplinary products with quality. It must tailor its products to clients' unique missions, while evolving toward an integrated product line made of easily supported components, termed "architecture." And it must offer a range of operational services safely and efficiently.

As impossible as they might seem, such expectations are not unrealistic. On the contrary, they represent the reality of business pressures. To survive in a competitive world, an organization cannot afford to fail at any of these missions.

To summarize all of these challenges, we must define what we mean by the "performance" of the organization. Of course, every organization offers a unique product line, so performance must be defined at a level higher than specific deliverables. Performance might be summarized as follows:

Organizational performance is efficiency (through productivity improvements and cost savings) at routine operational tasks and effectiveness (reflected in quality, flexibility, customer focus, and innovation) on creative tasks, year after year, in a rapidly changing environment.

Unfortunately, few organizations are reliably performing well, year after year. The problem is not the people; any organization has a range of talents (typically a normal distribution). The problem is not resources; increasing the budget of the organization is likely to produce more of the same, not new kinds of results. And the problem isn't technology either; a new tool or technique will only make the organization more efficient at what it chooses to do, although what it chooses to do may not be sufficient to meet the expanded expectations of the business environment. The problem may be deeper than any of these. The problem just may be an obsolete organization.

Organizations designed to do a good job in past decades typically are not equipped to address the challenges of today's business environment.

I.S. functions are an excellent example of this shortfall. Most I.S. organizations were designed simply to build, maintain, and operate mainframe-based transactions processing systems. Later, support for personal computers and administrative office systems were added. These patchwork organizations have generally performed adequately by yesterday's standards, but are now struggling in the face of tougher demands.

It is easy to spot a well-designed, *healthy* organization. A healthy organization encourages a dynamic balance between its various missions, and elicits the best performance from every one of its members. A healthy organization automatically adapts to a changing world. In a supportive environment, everyone is a "process owner" who flexibly arranges help from the prior stage in order to satisfy the next stage of the process. People always look for efficiencies, as do entrepreneurs in a competitive market. People are customer focused because they clearly understand that they must compete to survive in their markets with their product line. And quality is a natural outcome because small groups of people are responsible for every aspect of producing specific products of the organization.

On the other hand, unhealthy organizations build conflicts into the very fabric of the work environment, and "burn people out." They create untenable jobs, fail to align the organization's efforts with clients' business needs, and waste significant management time resolving internal political issues.

Good people, adequate resources, and innovative technologies do little good in unhealthy organizations. As critical as organizations are to people's success, rarely have organizations been consciously designed to handle today's multiplicity of paradoxical objectives, and to maintain excellence in the face of rapidly changing business needs and advancing technologies.

Organizational health is so critical that it warrants a special position within an executive's change strategy. Any executive who wishes to improve people's performance should address organizational issues first.

2. What Is an Organization?

The term "organization" refers to any group of people working together to achieve a common and ongoing purpose (line of business) which benefits people outside of their profession. It may be a corporation or a company, a government agency, a family working on their farm, a volunteer association, or a union. The organization may seek to make a profit, or it may be not-for-profit.

An organization is different from a project team. Organizations are permanent, or at least intended to survive beyond a single project. A project team, on the other hand, is a temporary association of people who belong to different parts of an organization and agree to work together to achieve a specific deliverable. The project team disbands at the end of the project, while its members continue to work for their respective organizations.

Organizations exist within organizations. The scope of the organization is a matter of perspective. If you are the C.E.O. of a multinational corporation, your scope may include numerous autonomous companies as well as corporate staff functions. If you are the president of a company within that conglomerate, the relevant organization is the entire company. If you are the I.S. executive within that company, the organization you care most about is the I.S. department.

I.S. departments make excellent examples of organizations within an organization. They have most of the elements found in any business as a whole: manufacturing of both products and services, customer service and training, a diversity of types of engineers, the need for an integrated product line, sales and marketing functions, and intense competition. I.S. departments are a rich microcosm of entire businesses. They are at least as large and complex as other staff functions, and in many cases more complex than the company as a whole. As such, the I.S. function will be used as the example of a staff organization throughout this book.

Organizations exist to serve "markets" -- groups of clients who benefit from their activities. If the organization is a company, the market is made up of its customers who are external to the company. If the organization is a department within the company such as I.S., its market is, for the most part, comprised of the other employees of the company.

An organization must have all of the elements necessary to deliver a useful product. It must have functions that design, manufacture, service, and sell its products. Anything less than this is a "group" within an organization rather than a whole organization.

Using this definition, most *staff* functions (e.g., I.S., Human Resources, Finance, Administration) are complete organizations that sell a product line different than the products of the company as a whole. Most *line* organizations (such as Sales, Engineering, Manufacturing) are not complete organizations but rather "groups" within a larger organization that is the company, which in turn serves external customers.

It would be very difficult to offer organizational guidelines that apply both to entire corporations as well as to every small, single-function group within it. But by defining the term "organization" as complete business units, we are able to develop a theory of organizational structure that applies to a wide variety of types of businesses. From this perspective, an I.S. department and a company as a whole have much in common. Lessons learned in one type of business can then be applied more broadly, to help leaders at a variety of levels -- from staff groups to entire corporations -- design healthy organizations.

3. Why Organizations Exist

Why do organizations exist?

Put another way, why would an organization perform any better than an equal number of individuals, all acting independently?

One obvious answer is that the people within the organization work toward a common purpose. But is common purpose enough?

Picture a number of people who are not part of an organization, but who agree to work toward a common purpose. For example, imagine thousands of individuals agreeing to work independently to make cars. Would you really expect them to compete with Toyota? Or even a small firm such as Rolls Royce?

A collection of individuals with a common purpose cannot perform much better than completely unrelated individuals. Just agreeing on a common purpose is not enough. If it were, we might as well ask every individual in a company to design, manufacture, and sell the company's products (as well as arrange for financial resources and build the necessary computer systems) all on their own.

Getting a number of people to agree to work toward a common purpose solves the problem of quantity, but not of complexity. For very simple tasks, it may be enough. For example, 100 people agreeing to pick up garbage along a stretch of roadside may perform nearly as well as an organization of 100 members. This is because each individual is fully capable of picking up garbage; more than one person is needed only to handle the necessary volume.

However, one person cannot make an entire car. To make a car alone, one person would have to be an expert at virtually every branch of design, engineering, procurement, manufacturing, distribution, finance, sales, etc. No one person can possibly know enough about all of these things.

We all know that one person cannot do everything. There is a scientific way to explain this obvious truth -- a concept that will help explain the reason organizations exist and identify the determinants of organizational performance.

Cybernetics, i.e., systems science, is the study of the control of complex, dynamic systems. A simple example is the thermostat in your home which turns on the heater when it gets too cold and the air conditioner when it gets too hot.

In the science of cybernetics the term "variety" is defined as the range of possible states of the system at any point in time. It is the complexity inherent in the many disciplines and day-to-day activities of the organization, multiplied by the pace of that activity (i.e., volume of activity per day):

$$VARIETY \ = \ COMPLEXITY \ x \ PACE$$

Variety is a measure of the throughput, or bandwidth, of an individual or organization -- one's ability to process information and perform activities in a given period of time.

Each individual is limited in his or her variety-handling capacity. A person can only think so many thoughts in a day, read so much, and know so much; that is, he or she can only process so much variety. For example, an executive cannot know every decision made by each employee each day, since one executive cannot process as much variety as the many people that comprise the organization.

An organization is confronted with tremendous variety. Think of all the knowledge within any one profession, and all the news of emerging techniques and technologies that a professional must keep up with. Then, multiply that complexity by all the many disciplines involved in making a car. Finally, multiply all that by the pace of events around that globe that affect a car manufacturer's business. This level of variety is unthinkable for any one individual.

It's a fundamental truth that people are limited in their variety-processing abilities. The question is, what can one do with a finite capacity for variety? People can use their finite variety-processing ability to know a little bit about everything -- the generalist who is a "jack of all trades and master of none." But then they would never know enough about any one field to master it, and certainly not enough to build a car.

On the other hand, specialists use their variety-processing abilities to learn one profession in depth. Of course, in order to work with others, specialists must use a little bit of their variety-processing abilities to know a little about everything else. With that caveat, by focusing on one field of study, specialists become very good at one thing.

Then, when specialists cooperate with each other by forming an organization, the organization has both depth and breadth. Organizations only perform better than individuals to the extent that they permit specialization. Said another way, organizations exist specifically to allow people to specialize. Within some practical limits, *the more that people specialize, the more depth they achieve and the better the organization can perform.*

But wait! There's a catch....

Imagine an organization made of specialists, all of whom are very good at their respective professions, but each of whom acts independently without coordination. How well would this organization perform?

Terribly! Actually, it would do worse than a collection of independent generalists. Since no one specialist sees the big picture, collectively they would be unlikely to get any products out the door.

Here's the catch: The more people specialize, the more they become interdependent. Put simply, *specialization depends on teamwork.*

Some people believe that organizations should be structured so as to reduce the need for teamwork, to "minimize hand-offs." If people within an organization are not good at forming teams across organizational boundaries, then they cannot afford to specialize. Each small group must replicate all of the skills that it is likely to need to avoid dependence on others. This is sometimes called the "stovepipe" organization, since it is made up of a set of self-sufficient groups of generalists that do not work well together -- like a bunch of vertical pipes that never touch. Of course, such organizations forego the advantages of their size and perform no better than a number of small companies. They might as well be broken up by a leveraged buy-out (or in the case of a staff function, decentralized).

Conversely, the better the organization is at teamwork, the more it can afford to specialize. Indeed, *the gating factor in many organizations is not money or people, but the mechanisms that coordinate people on teams.*

Coordination among specialists, then, is essential to organizational performance -- in fact, to the very existence of organizations.

Therefore, coordinating mechanisms (processes that build teamwork) are as important as the organization chart in building healthy, high-performance organizations. For this reason, any approach to organizational structure must address both the division of labor (the organization chart which determines people's specialties) and the coordinating mechanisms (which define work flows and combine people from throughout the organization on project teams to accomplish an organization's various objectives).

High-performance teamwork means more than just a willingness to work together. Teams must form quickly, and combine just the right specialized skills to address the challenge at hand. And effective collaboration depends on self-managing teams that work well without a lot of management intervention.

To ensure that teams form quickly, an organization cannot afford to wait for top management to decide when teams are needed and who should be on them. Top management cannot process enough variety to know every collaborative relationship needed throughout the organization. High-performance teamwork depends on *self-forming teams* that automatically ripple across the organization.

And to ensure self-managing teams, it must be absolutely clear who is to do what, and who has authority over whom. "All for one and one for all" may sound nice, and may indeed work if all of the team members are generalists. But in teams of specialists, differentiating people's roles is essential. And once responsibilities are separated, the team must somehow ensure that the various pieces of its work come together to produce the whole product.

Self-managing teams are built on the *differentiated roles and crystal clear flow of accountability* within the team.

There is one final ingredient to high-performance teamwork: *trust.* People must trust their peers within the organization to deliver what they promise, or else they won't risk depending on them. If people don't depend on each other, they will replicate each other's skills to be self-sufficient, and will slip back into a stovepipe organization.

Trust is earned. It is built on a track record of delivering on promises, and never promising what one cannot deliver. To ensure this level of reliability, each group within the organization must clearly understand its commitments, and must be empowered to manage these commitments.

In summary, **organizations exist in order to allow people to** *specialize...*

> **which in turn depends on** *teamwork...*

>> **which in turn depends on** *self-forming teams,*
>> *clear flows of accountability,* **and**
>> **business practices that engender** *trust.*

Therefore, to design a healthy structure, one must simultaneously design the organization chart and the coordinating processes that make teams work.

SO WHAT'S
THE PROBLEM?

4. Why Organizations Are Struggling

Most organizational structures have evolved over many years under a variety of executives. Structural adjustments were made to accommodate new technologies and services, special projects, and occasionally to handle personal career issues. Periodically, job descriptions and working relationships were changed as cyclic pressures for centralization and decentralization were felt. The resulting organizational structures seemed reasonable at the time, but now they may, in fact, be haphazard and dysfunctional.

As we've described, the purpose of an organization is to process more variety than individuals alone can handle. But most organizations evolved in a much simpler, lower-variety period of time. Now, the variety surrounding organizations is exploding.

Consider the following sources of variety:

*   Economic volatility instantly ripples around the world.

*   Rapidly changing political boundaries and alliances (e.g. the fall of the Soviet block and turmoil in Eastern Europe) bring new opportunities as well as threats.

*   The globalization of markets and competition means that current events anywhere in the world can affect the organization, adding to complexity. For example, the European Union and North American Free Trade Association dramatically changed the competitive environment.

*   Increasingly complex legal and regulatory restrictions are putting new, often conflicting, demands on organizations.

*   Clients are demanding customized service at the price of mass production, impacting the pace of product development by orders of magnitude.

* Technological complexity is multiplying in every field. In computing, for example, new generations of microprocessors and operating systems appear yearly, and some products (such as laptop computers) are obsoleted within months.

* Strategic partnerships are breaking down the boundaries between organizations, presenting new collaborative opportunities and problems.

* As the size of organizations grows, the number of possible collaborative relationships between people grows exponentially, further adding to the complexity of the work environment.

These changes in the business environment are matched by an accelerated pace of change at every level within organizations. It all adds up to a level of variety that challenges the capabilities of today's organizations.

If the only problem were the need for increased speed and flexibility, an effective response might be to break the organization up into small, autonomous business units. However, doing so reduces the degree of specialization, making the organization less capable of dealing with complexity.

If the only problem were increased complexity, an organization might partition itself into highly focused groups of specialists and expand the management hierarchy to coordinate them. But this is expensive, and can jeopardize the organization's ability to get work done quickly and flexibly.

If the only problem were cost, an organization might eliminate layers of management and simplify its processes. But as the management hierarchy is reduced, so are the coordinating mechanisms in the organization. As a result, it becomes difficult to adapt to a changing environment with flexible, cross-functional work processes. And as processes are simplified, the organization becomes more rigid (like an assembly line) and less capable of dealing with rapidly changing business demands.

The real problem is the combination of the need for speed and flexibility, specialization (to handle complexity), and efficiency and cost effectiveness. These factors add up to (actually, they *multiply* to) an explosion in variety that is taxing the limits of current organizations. Under the onslaught of variety, many cannot keep up. They find they are unable to simultaneously respond quickly and flexibly to customers' needs, innovate throughout their product lines, and operate in a cost-effective and reliable manner.

Some say an organization must choose whether it will focus on customer responsiveness, technical excellence, or operational efficiency. In fact, there is no reason why an organization cannot be world-class at all of these things. But to do so, they will have to learn to handle much more variety.

Simply patching old structures to accommodate new functions and technologies no longer works. New types of organizations are required. By their nature, these new organizations must engender high-performance teamwork among a wide range of both business and technology specialists, without regard to internal boundaries. They must be self-adjusting, to adapt to a rapidly changing environment. They must be highly responsive, dynamic, and customer focused; yet they must evolve toward a stable vision of an integrated product line. In short, organizations must be as well designed as the products they build.

5. How to Recognize Structural Problems

When things are not going well, it is all too easy to blame individuals for poor performance. However, even the best people will prove disappointing if structural problems impede their performance. Until structural issues are examined, one cannot really determine whether or not individuals are the root cause of the problem.

To decipher structural problems from people problems, executives have to recognize the kinds of problems that have their root cause in organizational structure. The following problems are common symptoms of faults in an organization's structure:

*   **Lack of strategic partnership with clients:** "Clients don't understand the strategic potential of our products, and don't invite us to participate in their planning processes. We are a passive utility that is here to deliver only what is asked of us."

    If an organization does no more than respond to requests for its products and services, clients will never learn to request anything other than what they've bought in the past. Unfortunately, in many cases, this means low-payoff administrative tools rather than mission-critical solutions. As a result, some clients fail to gain the real advantage of the products they buy. (For example, they use personal computers simply as expensive calculators and continue to buy enhancements to existing administrative solutions.) In extreme cases, clients oppose a proposed change and will not cooperate with the organization's implementation efforts.

    Of course, clients don't intentionally pass up strategic pay-offs or resist those who help them achieve their goals. They simply may not know any better.

    It is not clients' responsibilities to understand the importance of an organization's product line. Organizations must earn their appreciation through a track record of delivering mission-critical results, and they must take their fates into their own hands and ensure that results are indeed strategic.

The organization must do more than just deliver its products. It must proactively build clients' perception of the strategic use of its products; help clients find "breakthrough" opportunities; and offer the widest range of alternative solutions to ensure a match with clients' needs.

Technology experts (such as I.S. applications developers) are not the right people to help clients find strategic opportunities. They lack the business background and the time to study strategic needs-assessment methods.

Furthermore, it is not fair to ask technology experts to determine business requirements. This is a conflict of interests. Since they are specialists in just one type of solution -- their particular technology -- they cannot diagnose business needs without a bias for a predetermined solution. (For example, I.S. applications developers are paid to be biased in favor of transactions processing.)

Senior managers are no better qualified. They also lack the time to study the methods and to be with their clients, and most face the same conflict of interests.

This conflict of interests is a critical issue. Clients may require any of a broad range of solutions, drawing from the organization's entire product line. It takes just the right combination of tools to solve today's business challenges and maximize the organization's contribution to the bottom line. But experts in one product line (e.g. in I.S., mainframe applications or personal computers) are unlikely to offer unbiased recommendations. Clients recognize this, and mistrust staff groups who they perceive as "selling technology" rather than solving their business problems.

Before an organization can partner with clients at the strategic level, it must have an unbiased "consultancy" group that is not associated with any particular technology. Only an independent, dedicated group will have the time to professionalize client-oriented problem-finding (sales) methods, and the time to spend with clients.

While few companies lack sales and marketing functions, many staff organizations do. (For example, many I.S. departments have not organized an independent business consultancy.) Simply adding a client-liaison group to an existing organization has rarely worked. The only lasting solution is a comprehensive restructuring.

* **Clients unwilling to be open with the organization:** "Our clients treat us as outsiders rather than part of their management teams. They mistrust us and are reluctant to share information."

This symptom is generally recognized as a problem only in staff organizations within companies (such as an I.S. department).

Clients and staff organizations should work together for their mutual benefit and for the good of the company as a whole. Collaboration between technology specialists and client managers (who know how to run their businesses) is a prerequisite to utilizing the organization's products in strategic ways.

Poor organizational structure may preclude good partnership by defining staff jobs as controlling clients rather than serving them, or instructing people to look after technologies rather than people.

* **Pressure for decentralizaton or outsourcing:** "Our clients would rather do it themselves or hire our competitors than do business with us."

This is a severe symptom of the need for transformation.

Decentralization and outsourcing both represent a "loss of market share" for a staff function that serves as a business within a business. Loss of share may be the result of an organization's poor performance, its lack of customer focus, or an internal economy that doesn't give clients real control over priorities (their purchase decisions). But whatever the root cause, the organization's future survival is at stake.

Many organizations lack a client liaison function, and do a poor job of "sales and marketing" for lack of professional attention to their client-facing functions. And people throughout many organizations do not view clients as customers, but rather feel that their job is to do whatever they think is best for the company. (This is often caused by jobs defined as bureaucratic territories instead of lines of business.)

Again, the right answer is a fundamental analysis of organizational structure.

* **Slow pace of innovation:** "All my job allows me to do is crank out day-to-day work. I don't have the time (or permission) to explore new developments in my profession."

To succeed in business requires two types of innovation: continual evolution of current product lines, and a broadening into new products. Staying current is necessary to stay in business. And a diversity of products is necessary to tailor solutions to people's unique, mission-specific requirements.

I.S. provides a dramatic example of the expansion of product lines. I.S. staff functions in the past dealt with a relatively narrow range of technologies -- mainframes for transactions processing and P.C.s for office systems. Now, they are expected to provide expertise in all of the many specialized disciplines that affect the way a company manages information -- disciplines as diverse as micros, minis, mainframes, data communications, voice communications, teleconferencing, management science, library science, artificial intelligence, neural networks, computer-integrated manufacturing, image processing, multimedia, etc. The list is ever expanding.

To retain one's skill level and motivation, one must continually study one's profession as well as apply those skills to daily work. Without innovation, quality suffers and the organization risks becoming a solution in search of a problem -- a very poor business strategy.

Often we find that those who are supposed to be agents of change are the most resistant to change. They may even see it as their mission to protect their clients and the organization from change.

A slow pace of innovation indicates something built into the organizational design that encourages people to look after stability at the sacrifice of innovation.

Some organizational structures only accommodate experts in traditional products -- in I.S., mainframe-based transactions processing and end user computing -- and have not identified accountability for the many emerging product lines. Structure discourages continual learning when it defines jobs with no responsibility for research, planning, and professional development.

Even worse, structure may put people in a conflict-of-interests situation, being held responsible for both operational stability and technology innovation. Such a conflict of interests indicates a serious structural problem.

* **Fragmentation, and lack of integration:** "My job is to build good solutions, and standards only get in the way." Alternatively, "My project should determine the future architecture for the entire market (i.e., company)."

It's too easy for people to focus strictly on their current projects without regard for the broader issues of integration. There's always a reason to do a project a bit differently; but ultimately results are measured in terms of the organization's ability to support and integrate the solution as well as its immediate parochial benefits.

Architectural standards allow people to satisfy today's needs while evolving toward an integrated network of solutions. Architectural standards must encompass every specialty within the organization, and allow everyone to respond independently to clients' needs and yet still integrate their products.

No single specialty should drive architectural decisions alone, not even within their area of specialty, since others throughout the organization will have to live with the consequences. Therefore, good architectural decisions are based on a consensus of all of the specialists and service providers affected by the decision.

This participative approach requires ongoing attention. Unfortunately, many organizations lack an unbiased facilitator of multi-disciplinary architecture planning. As a result, standards are set haphazardly, perhaps without the involvement of the right stakeholders, or only when the need for a standard becomes obvious to top management.

When structure is missing a key element such as an architect, a reliable process is unlikely and fragmentation results.

* **Confused accountabilities, territorial disputes, empire building, and other management headaches:** "I spend so much of my time in meetings resolving internal disputes and making sure the organization works that I hardly have time to do my job or think strategically."

Finger pointing and territorial battles are among the most emotional of political issues. They generally involve lack of clarity or overlaps in structural boundaries.

Empire building is often rooted in the job-grading system. It may lead people to believe that the way to get more status, a better title, and salary increases is to control a bigger budget and more staff, even though the company is trying to control costs. People do what they are rewarded for (empire building), and rarely respond altruistically to platitudes about cost control.

In either case, a healthy structure and well-defined career paths will address the root cause and save leaders a lot of time.

* **Lack of teamwork:**   "That's your job, not mine. I'm not going to divert my efforts and take personal risk to help you."

All of the groups within an organization must work closely together to deliver integrated results. High-performance teamwork is more than a matter of team spirit. Unfortunately, in many organizations, teamwork is the exception rather than the rule.

Teamwork suffers when boundaries overlap or are unclear. In these circumstances, territorial friction stresses people's relationships and their ability to work together.

Also, in some organizations, cooperating with peers means taking a risk that you will not meet your own objectives. This occurs when the organization's structure does not align the objectives of the various groups within it. In such cases, groups may feel that doing their job means serving clients outside the organization, and not other groups within the organization who may also be legitimate customers.

In a well-planned structure, all boundaries are clear and distinct, and internal customers are recognized and given as much respect as clients outside the organization.

* **Demotivated people, or an anti-management sentiment:** "There's no way for me to have much impact on this organization, or to get ahead in this company. I'm just putting in my time."

There are many causes of a demotivated or even antagonistic work force, and a number of them are structural.

People are motivated when they feel in control of their work, proud of their accomplishments, and appreciated. However, may structures disempower people, discourage a feeling of "ownership" of a part of the business, and fail to reward them for their accomplishments.

Structure may define jobs in terms of tasks and responsibilities, rather than lines of business. Without a vision of the end result, people have no basis for identifying new ways to do things better or for inventing entirely new products and services. So, day after day, they just go on doing the tasks they've been given without thinking creatively about the future. In such cases, structure does not permit empowerment or entrepreneurship.

For those at the beginning of their careers, the situation may be even more bleak. In some cases, a combination of structure and Human Resources policies conspire to reward generalists over specialists, constraining technical experts to low-level jobs and salaries. If the only way to get ahead is as a manager and people's jobs don't prepare them for management, there is little hope of advancement. When the structure does not provide technical career paths, technical people feel unrewarded and have little reason to excel.

The structure should be designed to provide empowered, entrepreneurial jobs for people with either technical or managerial interests.

Each of these problems may be traced directly to the structure of an organization. It would do little good to address them with cultural statements, methods, or technologies. It certainly doesn't do any good to blame people who respond to organizational influences and do exactly what they are paid to do. The only effective answer is restructuring.

6. Structures that Don't Work

Executives have experimented with a wide variety of structural forms that have solved some problems while creating others. Some are amusing; others sadly familiar. Many attempt to use structure to avoid the need for collaboration and teamwork, or as a substitute for an effective, client-driven priority-setting process.

Experimentation is expensive. Executives can avoid repeating the mistakes of the past by studying others' failures. We also can draw from past experiences principles that guide the design of healthy organizations.

Among the many organizational structures that frequently fail are:

* **Organizing technology experts by client area:** Each client gets a little group of generalists who cannot perform as well as teams of specialists. Meanwhile, reinvention, inconsistent directions, and fragmented results are to be expected. The organization might as well be decentralized, since it is not taking advantage of the synergies of being one integrated organization.

* **Assigning people two bosses (one the customer, the other providing technical direction) in a matrix organization:** Clients get only those technologies which their groups know, and have difficulty getting help from other kinds of specialists (because they are dedicated to other clients). Also, even if the customer's new project requires a different mix of skills, the organization cannot be restructured whenever a new project arises. As a result of this inflexibility, projects are not staffed with the people best qualified to do them.

*   **Assigning client liaison responsibility to senior managers:**
    No one has enough time to spend with clients, or to perfect the
    methods of strategic needs assessment. Furthermore, senior
    managers have biases originating from the specific product lines
    their groups represent, so they do a poor job of offering clients
    unbiased business advice. As a result, strategic opportunities
    are lost and partnerships suffer.

*   **Organizing technology developers by clients' business
    strategies:**   Since clients are involved in multiple business
    strategies, they must diagnose their needs before knowing
    whom to call. As a result, the organization is left out of the
    clients' critical early thinking, and partnerships suffer. Also,
    for problems that affect multiple strategies (e.g., personal
    effectiveness), there's no one to call.

*   **Organizing technology experts by clients' business
    processes:**   Clients must diagnose their needs on their own to
    know which process expert to call, and they have no one to call
    for needs other than those related to the few identified business
    processes. Furthermore, since a variety of client processes
    may share the same needs (e.g. in I.S., many processes may
    use the same data), the process-oriented experts reinvent
    solutions with potential inconsistencies and higher costs.

*   **Organizing all technology developers strictly by application
    domain** (e.g. in I.S., financial, manufacturing and
    administrative applications):   There's no room in the
    organization for applications-independent (client-purpose-
    independent) specialists, so everybody must learn for
    themselves and reinvent these other skills. (In I.S., for
    example, there is no place for specialists in computing
    platforms, information engineering, end user computing, and
    other disciplines.)

*   **Organizing product developers by delivery platform** (e.g. in I.S., by desk-top versus mainframe computer platforms): Developers naturally are biased in favor of their given platforms, and there's no one to look after innovation in new platforms or cross-platform approachs (e.g., client-server applications).

*   **Separating product development and maintenance groups:** This requires two of every expert, which reduces specialization and hence performance. There is little incentive to do things right the first time, so costs rise. And, the two "classes of citizenship" lead to morale problems.

*   **Separating long- and short-term development groups:** This builds internal competition, and encourages clients to buy "quick and dirty" solutions that may be difficult to maintain.

*   **Separating project managers and the worker (programmer) pool:** The workers in the pool make many key design decisions as they do the detailed development work, although for lack of specialization they are limited in their depth of knowledge of the applications. As a result, productivity is low and quality suffers. Also, the worker pool is a dead-end job that generates serious morale problems.

*   **Forming a project managers pool:** Project managers have a limited understanding of applications because of their lack of specialization, and may lead teams to make poor design decisions. Also, as they rotate from project to project, project managers build little sense of ownership of any product line, reducing their commitment to quality.

*   **Representing projects in the formal structure**, rather than defining project teams that cut across boundaries: The organization must be restructured whenever major projects end. Also, people in project groups worry about their next job, and may prolong projects unnecessarily or spend an inordinate amount of time searching for their next job. Meanwhile, smaller projects cannot use this approach, so they may lack the specialists they need.

* **Forming a "quality control" function:** The inspectors relieve everyone else of their responsibility for quality, so people generate more defects. This leads to lower quality and higher costs due to the need for rework.

* **Forming an "emerging technologies R&D" or a "strategic planning" group:** Concentrating responsibility for learning in one small group takes away from everyone else the responsibility for thinking about the future, and puts everyone else in dead-end jobs. It also creates a bottleneck for learning that actually slows the pace of innovation.

* **Combining responsibility for design and operations:** Keeping things running means keeping things stable, so little innovation occurs. In I.S., for example, experts in hardware platforms are often placed under those who operate the computers. Since new generations of platforms (e.g., client-server) disrupt smooth operations, little progress is made.

* **Depending on a culture of teamwork or defined processes in an amorphous structure:** People don't know what they're supposed to be good at, so everybody follows their personal interests, and gaps and overlaps in knowledge occur. Also, teamwork suffers since it's not clear where to turn for help in any given specialty.

These cases show how painful poorly designed structures can be.

THE SCIENCE OF
ORGANIZATIONAL DESIGN

7. How Structure Affects People

Despite an ever growing body of historical evidence, some still believe that formal structure has little real impact. Rather, they believe the "informal organization" really determines how things get done. In their view, success depends on good people, motivated by a culture of teamwork, who altruistically think beyond their job descriptions and "do what's right."

It is possible for "superior" people motivated by an excellent leader and a spirit of teamwork to overcome structural dysfunctions. However, to do so, managers will have to waste their precious time dealing with the friction created by structural problems. On the other hand, these same people in a healthy structure would produce far higher levels of performance.

A brief story illustrates the powerful impact of organizational structure on performance.

A large airline divided its I.S. department into two computer centers: conventional I.S., and its reservations system. Reporting to each computer-center director was a systems-development manager.

On the conventional I.S. side, top management became very frustrated because the department retained an archaic mainframe. The systems-development manager had failed to implement a new platform, so they fired him for lack of technological innovation. Two years later, they fired the next systems-development manager for the same reason. Two years after that, still another manager was fired.

These systems-development managers were all bright, seasoned people who were good at their professions. The problem wasn't their lack of ability.

Consider this dilemma: You are this systems-development manager, and your boss is the computer-center director. He is paid to keep things running *reliably, safely, and cheaply.* Would you dare suggest a new mainframe? Of course not!

Your boss, head of computer operations, is rewarded for stability; and the implementation of a new platform (an "invention") inevitably disrupts operational stability. Since the boss is paid to resist change, the manager of systems development tasked with change is destined to fail.

This clearly is a structural problem. If an "invention" function reports to an operational function, little progress will occur -- no matter who has the job of invention. It is both futile and cruel to replace the systems-development manager for poor performance when the fault lies in the organizational structure.

Good organizational design does not rely on the altruism and above-average people. Clear roles give people a framework in which to exercise their entrepreneurial spirit. When well designed, structure allows people to act independently while automatically coordinating their activities. This empowerment taps everyone's talents. And it relieves management of responsibility for detailed supervision and problem resolution, allowing them to focus their time and energy on the strategic activities of the business.

A well-structured organization also enhances teamwork by assigning each group its own clearly defined area of specialty. From this foundation, people know where to turn for specific kinds of help, and teams are formed in response to customers' requirements. Projects tie people with clear and distinct charters together into cooperative teams. The result is a high degree of collaboration across well-defined structural boundaries.

The effects of structure are extremely powerful. Since it represents a stable guiding force, structure transcends time and the issues of the day. Thus, organizational structure has a significant impact on people's success -- in particular, on their ability to deliver strategic value, work in teams, integrate their activities, and grow and adapt.

A well-designed structure can guide people into their most effective roles, and ensure organizationwide teamwork. On the other hand, an unhealthy organizational structure can create unnecessary political stress and continually impede performance.

Certainly not all performance problems are structural, but organizational structure is one of the most critical determinants of performance. If the structure is dysfunctional, a brilliant vision, top-notch people, and plentiful resources will have little impact. Attempts to improve its performance will be frustratingly unprofitable. New methods, policies, technologies, and people won't help if the design of the organization impedes people's best efforts.

The power of organizational structure must not be underestimated. Put simply:

Good people in a poor organizational structure will fail, while average people in a healthy structure can succeed.

For this reason, structure is often the starting point for building a high-performance organization.

8. The Benefits of a Healthy Structure

What can an executive expect to gain by restructuring?

A healthy structure helps everyone succeed by virtue of its impacts upon three areas: job definitions, processes and teamwork, and culture:

*   Job definitions:

- Eliminates overlaps, redundant efforts, and territorial disputes.

- Provides people with clear direction on what it is at which they are supposed to excel.

- Makes sure that someone has the job of looking after every aspect of the organization's mission.

- Empowers people to be largely self managing.

- Flattens organizations, saving money and shortening communication paths.

- Builds whole jobs that are fulfilling and motivational.

- Eliminates impossible jobs that only "super-people" can fill.

- Balances conflicting objectives without creating jobs that put people in conflict-of-interests situations.

- Capitalizes on the diversity of all the people in the organization.

- Provides career paths for specialists as well as generalists.

* Processes and teamwork:

    - Allows a diversity of business processes to flexibly get the right talent doing the right things on each project team.

    - Ensures clear accountability within project teams.

    - Provides a mechanism for self-forming project teams.

    - Supports fundamental businesslike practices such as forming clear agreements and meeting all commitments.

    - Permits independent action to serve individual customers without a loss of integration (in I.S., inter-operable networks of systems) to serve clients' shared needs.

* Culture:

    - Focuses people on their customers (internal and external).

    - Focuses people on delivering results, not on bureaucratic territories, procedures, and tasks.

    - Builds a culture of entrepreneurship where people proactively explore new and better ways to satisfy their customers, and seek to minimize overhead rather than maximize their territories.

    - Establishes work practices which embody the objectives of Total Quality Management.

    - Automatically adjusts the organization to new technologies, service requirements, changes in clients' business, and evolution of its own processes.

9. A Systematic Approach to Structure

Everyone has an opinion about organizational structure, and people have experimented with a tremendous variety of approaches. The problems they intended to address are quite real. But with the many conflicting forces at work, it is all too easy to make subtle mistakes that solve some problems while creating many others.

The response may be yet another organizational experiment. Some executives repeatedly change their organization's structure -- one year decentralizing and the next recentralizing; now organizing by technologies and later by client groupings. In some cases, every new product or service requires a new organization. In the worst cases, whenever anything goes wrong, the executive restructures the organization again.

Repeated reorganization is highly disruptive and expensive. This "thrashing" -- the "organization *du jour*" -- is a symptom of the lack of a *model* of healthy organizational structure that addresses the diversity of organizational issues and provides a consistent evolutionary direction.

The definition of structural boundaries is more than a matter of clarifying territories to eliminate overlaps and give people a clear focus in their jobs. The organizational environment in which people work can be scientifically designed to maximize people's effectiveness and job satisfaction, and the overall performance of the organization.

Basing structural design on scientific principles and a model of the ideal achieves a number of extremely important objectives:

* It allows executives to solve organizational problems without creating new ones.

* It overcomes political biases, and allows organizations to take advantage of individual strengths without structuring around individual personalities.

* It helps executives communicate the various roles within the organization clearly to other executives, clients, and the organization's staff itself. Client executives better understand whom to call for what, and people throughout the organization better understand their roles and what it means to be excellent at their jobs. Furthermore, everyone gains a clearer understanding of everyone else's role and their interdependencies, nurturing an environment of collaboration and mutual supportiveness.

* It guides the organization toward consistent evolutionary change.

* It makes participation by people throughout the organization in the structural design process safe, shifting discussions from political combat to objective principles.

If it is good to base structural design on a scientific model of organizations, what makes for a good model?

An organizational model must transcend individual variables such as personality, intelligence, skill, and management style. It must apply to any organization, regardless of the particular skills and disciplines, technologies, projects, and strategies that seem to change so quickly. It must explain the broader patterns of diverse people working together to achieve a diversity of common purposes.

The science of cybernetics fulfills all of these objectives. When applied to organizations, cybernetics offers the following perspective:

Organizations can be viewed as a set of parallel but interlinked dynamic systems.

Stafford Beer, the British cybernetician, pioneered the application of systems science to organizational design. *1* NDMA applied Beer's thinking to a variety of organizations, and augmented theory with field research on the difficulties faced by many actual organizations in various states of disrepair and the attributes of successful organizations. What emerged was a model describing the workings of a high-performance organization, including specific principles that can guide executives in designing healthy organizational structures.

We term the model "Structural Cybernetics" because it views an organization as a dynamic system of interacting components, each responding to feedback from its organizational environment, and at the same time dynamically interacting with each other as part of a coherent system. The goal of Structural Cybernetics is to help leaders build high-performance organizations that are systematically designed to succeed.

In Structural Cybernetics, the purpose of the organizational chart is to form loci of expertise -- groups that represent entrepreneurships -- each a system in itself and at the same time an element of a larger system. Each entrepreneurship addresses a clearly focused set of objectives so as not to demand too much of individuals or put them in conflict-of-interests situations.

Because well-focused entrepreneurs must depend on others for other skills, the design of a healthy organizational structure must include both the division of labor (the organization chart that defines the various entrepreneurial groups) and processes which ensure teamwork across structural boundaries. In Structural Cybernetics, explicit mechanisms flexibly combine the well-focused entrepreneurs into teams that include all of the necessary talent to accomplish each project's unique objectives.

Structural Cybernetics includes four key elements:

1. Pragmatic principles of organizational design.

2. Clear definitions of the various functions within an organization -- the building blocks of structure -- that can be assembled into an organization chart.

3. Mechanisms for forming multi-disciplinary teams dynamically, i.e., the practicalities of the "network organization." In contrast to a stifling one-process-fits-all approach, this network of entrepreneurs empowers people to flexibly tailor processes to the business objectives at hand without any loss of efficiency or accountability.

4. A carefully planned implementation process that brings about paradigm shifts and dramatic cultural change along with a healthy structure in an open and participative manner.

The first two elements -- the principles of design and the building blocks of structure -- are used to design the organization chart. The third element -- flexible mechanisms of teamwork -- brings the organization chart to life by determining how work will get done. And, the fourth element -- the implementation process -- is critical to making the design a reality.

---

1.   Beer, Stafford. *The Heart of the Enterprise.* Chichester, UK: John Wiley & Sons. 1979. Page 7.

10. Principles of Healthy Structural Design

In Structural Cybernetics, the guiding principles of organizational design are drawn from three key sources:

*   The cybernetic principle of *feedback loops,* which must be both appropriate and comprehensive.

*   The cybernetic principle of *requisite variety,* which is the ability of every element in the organization to adequately handle all of the complexity it faces.

*   The characteristics of a *motivational environment.*

Appropriate Feedback Loops

One of the most basic tenets of cybernetics is that systems are controlled by feedback loops. In the example of the thermostat, the heater would not know how long to run were it not for the feedback loop embodied in the thermostat that measures temperature. In organizations, this key cybernetic concept can be described as follows:

People generally do what you reward them for doing.

This maxim is not intended to imply that managers and professionals will only do those tasks that they are explicitly paid to do and no more. But over the long term, people generally do what brings rewards, both extrinsic and intrinsic. The behaviors that are rewarded are defined in their job definitions and performance objectives. These are examples of feedback loops.

Feedback loops must be appropriate; that is, objectives and metrics must be consistent with what is expected of people. It is unfair to ask people to sacrifice their personal performance appraisals (and potentially those of their team members) for the sake of the clients' well-being.   Organizations based on altruism typically fall apart when the leader who inspired self-sacrifice moves on to another job.

This simple cybernetic principle of appropriate feedback loops leads to a number of organizational design principles:

1.   Define Clear Charters

A healthy structural design should provide a *crystal clear definition of the "business" of each group within the organization.*   It should provide people with clear direction on what it is at which they are supposed to excel.

2.   Define Distinct Charters

To build an atmosphere of cooperation and teamwork, the structure of the organization must ensure distinct charters. The structure must *clearly define unique product lines for every group within the organization.*   This will eliminate overlaps, redundant efforts, and territorial disputes.

3.   Define Comprehensive Charters

To ensure top performance on all of its missions, the organization must include a comprehensive set of "businesses." This means that the structure must *clearly define charters for every essential function within the scope of the organization.* It should explicitly place accountability for every aspect of the organization's mission, including stability of operations, technical invention, coordination and integration of activities, and business-driven change.

4. Avoid Conflicts of Interests

When feedback loops are unclear, ambiguous, or conflicting, the results will be unpredictable and less than optimal. Thus, another objective of healthy structure is to define jobs with consistent and nonconflicting objectives, and to *reserve conflicts of interests for the highest possible level of the organization.* This allows the organization to balance conflicting objectives without creating jobs that put people in conflict-of-interests situations.

5. Match Structure to Specialty

Similarly, the way in which a group's boundaries are defined sends signals that tell people what they are supposed to be good at. To send the right signals to people about their focus, *the bases for substructure should be determined separately for each of the various functions, and should match the primary specialty of each group.* In this way, the structure sends clear and consistent signals about each group's primary focus.

6. Pay for Results, Not Tasks

To align feedback loops with intended results, *structure should define jobs by the products they produce rather than the skills or tasks needed to produce them.* This focuses people on satisfying their customers, and builds whole jobs that are fulfilling and motivational.

7. Make Interdependencies Explicit

To ensure teamwork, interdependencies must be clearly established. To do so, structure should *build a clear understanding of each group's internal customers and suppliers.* Businesslike relationships among groups within an organization is a necessary ingredient for high-performance teamwork.

8. Build Forces for Integration

Healthy structural design explicitly assigns responsibilities for ensuring collaboration across technical boundaries. It *programs into the organization a force for both short- and long-term integration.* The structure must permit independent action in service of individual customers, without a loss of integration (e.g., inter-operable networks of information systems) to serve shared organizational needs.

9. Build Forces for Adaptation

A healthy structure *includes a function dedicated to improving the structure.* In this way, the structure is self-adjusting, accommodating new technologies, service requirements, changes in clients' business, and evolution of its own processes.

Requisite Variety

A second key cybernetic principle that applies to organizational structure is W. Ross Ashby's "Law of Requisite Variety." [2] Variety measures the ability of an individual or an organization to process information and events. Ashby observed that variety always balances. If it isn't done in a planned way, things will "fall through the cracks."

The limits to an individual's variety-handling capacity lead to a very important truth: If jobs require too much variety handling (requiring a super-person), executives are bound to be frustrated in their search to staff the position, and disappointed with whomever fills the job.

This same fact can be put another way:

People can only be world-class experts at one thing at a time.

People can be generally aware of many thing -- mediocre at more than one thing -- but only excellent at one specialty. Their areas of expertise may be big or small, depending on their capabilities. And people may rotate among specialties in the course of their careers. But at any point in time, one must concentrate on a well-defined area of expertise to remain competitive by world-class standards.

Structural design is equivalent to distributing the total variety-processing requirements of the organization among its members. For the purpose of structural design, the following additional principles result:

10. Avoid the Need for "Super-people"

Healthy structural design eliminates impossible jobs that only super-people can fill. The more the organizational structure permits specialization, the more depth it can offer in each area, and the better it will perform vis-a-vis its competition. To ensure the highest quality, the organization must be structured so that *each job only requires a single type of expertise, permitting a high degree of specialization.*

11. Avoid Jobs for Underachievers

A healthy organization *employs everyone's full range of talents within well-defined lines of business.* By doing so, it flattens the organization, and encourages people to be largely self managing.

12. Empower All Levels

In a healthy organization, every level is empowered, and concomitantly held accountable for results rather than tasks. Then, everybody can determine how they will accomplish their commitments, and what help they'll need. To get the most from everybody and provide everyone with career-enhancing opportunities, structure should *permit empowerment at every level.*

13. Empower All Functions

Not only should empowerment extend to every level; it should also extend to every function within the organization. In some unhealthy organizations, one group is given the authority while another has the accountability. This is prejudice against the function deprived of its authority. A healthy organizational structure links authority and accountability. It *empowers people in every function within the organization with all the authority, entrepreneurial freedom, and resources that they need to produce their products.*

Motivational Environment

Three additional guiding principles (derived from the vast literature on organizational behavior) describe the characteristics of an effective motivational environment:

14. Avoid Discrimination Against Functions

The organization must be equally ready to support any of its many lines of business without predefined preferences. But when the structure embodies prejudice against a functional area -- either by disempowering a line of business or assigning entire functions lower grade levels -- that function will not perform well. A common example is discrimination against functions that sell services rather than products. In I.S. for example, those who run the computer center may be considered lower status that those who develop new technologies. *Structural design must accommodate many peer entrepreneurships without a bias that places one above another.*

15. Design Around Personality Types, Not Individuals

The importance of a match between one's personality and one's job is evident to every experienced manager. On the other hand, organizations cannot be designed around individual personalities. When this is done, reorganization is required whenever anyone changes jobs. Furthermore, doing so often distorts the structure and creates untenable jobs for others in order to give someone a little more, or less, territory.

Personality must be viewed at a higher level. Healthy structural design seeks to identify personality archetypes, and match each broad category to the function. A well-designed structure will accommodate each individual with *jobs that require only a single personality archetype.* This capitalizes on the diversity of the people in the organization without the disruption that occurs when jobs are tailored to individuals.

16. Do Not Reward Empire Building

A healthy organizational structure and culture *eliminates all incentives for empire building.* Career paths are provided for technology specialists as well as generalists; supervisory responsibilities are just one job evaluation factor among many, and senior-level individual contributors have the same earnings opportunities as those who manage large groups.

---

2. Ashby, W. Ross. *An Introduction to Cybernetics.* Chapman and Hall. 1956.

THE BUILDING BLOCKS
OF STRUCTURE

11. The Functional Building Blocks
of Structure

To provide a basis for a structural design that achieves all of the guiding principles, we must first define the basic functions that every organization must accomplish. These functions comprise the building blocks of structure. (See Figure 1.) This functional framework is used to establish a language for analyzing organizational problems.

The functional building blocks are also used to design healthy structures, by assembling them into an organization chart in a manner that satisfies the unique needs of each organization. This organizational design process can be guided by the Structural Cybernetics principles listed in Chapter 10.

In this process, the functional building blocks ensure that every aspect of an organization's mission is assigned, and that people have clear and non-overlapping territories. In other words, every line of business within the organization should be within one, and only one, group's domain.

The functional building blocks of structure fall in five major categories:

* Technologists.
* Service Bureaus.
* Coordinators.
* Consultants.
* Audit.

Technologists

The products of the organization are designed by technology or discipline specialists -- the engineers. Structural Cybernetics calls them *Technologists*. This building block includes engineers and experts in the various disciplines involved in product design and operation. In I.S., this category includes:

* Applications development.
* Personal computing.
* End user computing (office systems, interactive tools for thinking, multimedia).
* Data telecommunications.
* Voice telecommunications, teleconferencing.
* Operations research/management science.
* Library science.
* Records management/archival services.
* Artificial intelligence, expert systems, neural networks, fuzzy logic.
* Image processing.
* Process control, computer integrated manufacturing.
* Computer aided software engineering.

Each type of Technologist has a specialty that is defined by its particular expertise. For example, each area of technology is a profession in itself, with its own journals, professional societies, conferences, theories, and methods.

As noted in Ashby's Law of Requisite Variety, it is impossible for most people to be a world-class expert at more than one thing at a time. One can be an expert in one technology and broadly aware of others. But a Technologist asked to support more than one discipline will find it extremely difficult to excel at his or her job, no matter how bright and hard working he or she may be.

Excellence in the design of complex products requires teams of specialists collaborating on projects, rather than a few generalists attempting to do everything in isolation.

There are two major categories of Technologists: "Applications" and "Base."

We use the term "Applications Technologist" to mean those who produce purpose-specific products, that is, solutions designed to address one and only one type of problem. In I.S., this means "data-specific software," typically routine, well-structured transactions processing systems. It includes both business applications (D.P./M.I.S.) and process control applications. It is distinguished from the term "tools," which refers to end user computing.

Base Technologists are specialists in disciplines and technologies that are *not* purpose-specific. They may tailor their products to particular clients and purposes; but even without tailoring, the product should be useful to many kinds of clients to solve many kinds of problems.

In I.S., there are five subcategories of Base Technologies:

* **Platforms:**   personal computers, minicomputers, mainframes, systems software, input/output devices, database management systems (and physical data modeling), voice and data telecommunications, and network engineering.

   Platforms include both hardware (computers, devices, instruments) and environmental software (operating systems, system utilities, schedulers, graphical user interfaces, system monitoring and tuning tools, and security tools).

* **Technologists science:**   tools and methods specific to the profession of the organization's Technologists. In the case of I.S., this includes software engineering and computer science tools and methods such as computer-aided software engineering (C.A.S.E.) tools, systems development life-cycle (S.D.L.C.) methods, information engineering, and electronic data

interchange (E.D.I.). Software engineering includes methods and tools that are specific to the practice of computer science, as well as software library routines and data encoding techniques. All the knowledge of Base Technologists is common to more than one area of technology.

* **End user computing tools:** word processing, outline editors, electronic publishing, spreadsheets and decision support systems, graphics, multimedia, calendars and project management tools, data query and bulletin boards, electronic mail, computer conferencing, voice message systems, and teleconferencing. End user computing includes the wide range of interactive "tools for thinking," which are implemented on a variety of platforms (not just personal computers).

* **Profession-specific tools:** computer aided design (C.A.D.), computer aided engineering (C.A.E.), and scientific computing. Scientific, technical, and engineering tools are specialized end user computing tools designed for a specific profession, but excludes tools specific to the profession of the Technologists. (If this area is small, profession-specific tools may be considered part of end user computing.)

* **Disciplines:** information professions that are not hardware and software related, but rather specialize in methods for information handling (again not specific to the profession of the Technologists). Examples include management science, artificial intelligence, neural networks, fuzzy logic, library science, and records management.

Service Bureaus

Another familiar set of staff functions is termed *Service Bureaus.* Service Bureaus are dedicated to providing operational services reliably and efficiently -- they deliver the manufacturing and support services.

There are two different types of Service Bureaus: "Machine-based" and "People-based."

Machine-based Service Bureaus own and operate shared-use machines. The services they sell are primarily produced by machines, and the people are there to ensure that the machines run properly. This is the manufacturing function of the organization. In I.S., this means infrastructure and systems used by people throughout the company, including the computer center, telecommunications network operations, and the telephone system.

Machine-based Service Bureaus buy the equipment in their factories (from Technologists). In I.S., this includes computing and telecommunications platforms. They own and operate this equipment to produce services for others. Operations includes adjusting the parameters built into the solutions, and following procedures for their use and problem resolution. But if any changes to the design of the solution are needed, Service Bureaus buy help from Technologists.

There are three types of functions which are categorized as People-based Service Bureaus:

1. People-based Service Bureaus provide *services produced by people rather than machines.* Equipment, such as computers, is employed only to make the people more productive at tasks they conceivably could do manually. These services can, in turn, be divided into two categories:

    1a. Services to clients that enhance the organization's primary product line. The most common example is customer support (help desk or hotline).

1b. Services to others within the organization to leverage their time and enhance their abilities. Examples include technician services (e.g., routine installations and repairs), professional writing, project management consulting, and internal administration.

2. The organization may also have a few other relatively small functions that can be considered "staff to staff." These are entire businesses-within-a-business that produce goods and services not specifically part of the organization's product line. Examples include education services, internal finance, and internal human resources. If the organization chooses to hire its own professionals rather than buy services from a peer staff function, these professionals would be classed as People-based Service Bureaus.

These other functions might be considered separate organizations in their own right. When the organization is defined as a very large entity (e.g., the whole firm), these staff functions may be large enough to include all of the building blocks, and the entire Structural Cybernetics model and process may be applied. Nonetheless, from the perspective of the broader organization, they are considered People-based Service Bureaus.

People-based Service Bureaus may maintain a locus of expertise as Technologists do, but their specialty is outside the mainstream of the organization. For example, education, graphic arts, project management, and quality are all specialties in themselves. However, these specialists do not directly produce the products and services of the organization (e.g., information systems). Their role is indirect; they help others in the organization produce the product line. And, although they are specialists in other fields, they are still considered People-based Service Bureaus rather than Technologists.

Both types of Service Bureaus seek continuous improvements on the margin, but are not generally proponents of major changes which disrupt their operational efficiency. Service Bureau professionals are not promoted on the basis of their inventions, but rather for their responsiveness, reliability, security, low cost, and attention to detail. They efficiently manage large capital budgets and many people.

Two Familiar Functions, Two Missing Functions

While companies as a whole are generally better balanced, most traditional staff organizations are comprised only of Technologists (e.g., I.S. applications developers and P.C. experts) and Service Bureaus (e.g., the I.S. computer center and network operations).

In these structures, no one short of the executive is responsible for integrating all of the Technologists' perspectives into an architectural plan or a business plan. Similarly, organizational plans and research endeavors lack necessary coordination.

Furthermore, no one is responsible for the unbiased diagnosis of the clients' business needs. This is because many organizations lack a business-oriented professional who is not associated with any one product line. Similarly, no one is tasked with integrating a variety of specialists onto project teams to build complex solutions that require multiple technologies (such as multi-function and cooperative-processing information systems).

The traditional organizational structure of staff functions performed adequately in its day, but as the challenges facing the business have grown, it has proven inadequate.

Two critical pieces are missing from this conventional structure: The Architect and other Coordinators (such as planners and facilitators), and Consultancies.

The Architect

One of the most critical challenges of an organization is to bring together many disparate technologies and disciplines, applied to a diversity of projects, into an integrated product line (in I.S., a network of solutions, tools, and databases).

In the past, integration was assured by designing large systems from the top down. Technologists analyzed a set of business problems, designed a comprehensive solution, and then built it piece by piece. Years later when the total solution was complete, its integration was guaranteed since every piece of it was designed at the same time. In this historic context, architecture was considered the first stage of design.

Top-down planning worked well when the organization was addressing relatively stable problems. For example, this is the way I.S. departments planned integrated administrative applications such as order processing and financial accounting. These were business processes that didn't change significantly over the period of time required to build the comprehensive system.

Now, however, most organizations are addressing problems directly linked to business strategy, and the strategic business environment is anything but stable. To remain viable, companies have to be flexible, responsive, and agile. To remain aligned with strategy, every organization within a company must do the same.

The traditional "top-down, design-and-build" approach is far too rigid and inflexible to adapt to the rapidly changing strategies of today's business environment. By the time these grand designs are completed, the resulting solutions are no longer relevant, and the intended clients have moved on to other frontiers (or even other jobs).

In the strategic era, architecture is not the first step in systems design. It is not something that is planned and then built. Architecture planning must not be another attempt to design solutions from the top down. To the contrary, the very purpose of architecture is to allow opportunistic, business-driven implementation efforts while still evolving toward an integrated product line.

Architecture is a set of standards, guidelines, and statements of direction that constrain the design of solutions for the purpose of eventual integration.

In I.S., for example, there are numerous types of architectural standards, including decisions about computing platforms by level of network, functionality by level of network, telecommunications protocols, data interchange standards, information resource management, cooperative-processing protocols, and supporting materials. All of these types of standards must be represented in an architectural framework before the architecture can provide comprehensive guidance to implementors.

The architectural plan must encompass all of the component technologies, without a bias for any one. For this reason, the architecture planning process must not be driven by any one technical domain or group of Technologists.

In some organizations, an individual or small group is given responsibility for the development of the architecture plan, that is, for decisions on standards. This is a mistake. By its very nature, architecture impacts the work of all of the various technical specialists. Therefore, architectural standards must be based on technical trends in all of the Technologists' areas. But no single person or small group can track so many technologies with competence (as per Ashby's Law of Requisite Variety).

Furthermore, when one small group makes all the decisions, it is unlikely to gain the "buy in" of the Technologists who will implement the architecture and the Service Bureaus who must live with the results.

Architecture, in its best sense, is a *shared vision* among all of those affected by a standard of how their various products will be tied

The Building Blocks of Structure

Consultants

STRATEGIC	**RETAIL**	**MARKETING**
ACCOUNT EXECUTIVES, DIRECT SALES TO MAJOR ACCOUNTS	THE STOREFRONT, AVAILABLE TO ANYONE ON DEMAND	ONE-TO-MANY COMMUNICATIONS

Coordinators

ARCHITECT	**PLANNERS**	**ORGANIZATIONAL EFFECTIVENESS**	**RESEARCH COORDINATOR**
FACILITATES CONSENSUS ON STANDARDS THAT ENCOURAGE INTEGRATION	HELPS EVERYONE DEVELOP BUSINESS PLANS AND DISASTER RECOVERY PLANS	HELPS EVERYONE DEVELOP EFFECTIVE ORGANIZATIONS	GIVES OUT GRANTS TO ALLOW EVERYONE TO DO RESEARCH IN THEIR FIELDS

Technologists

APPLICATIONS	**BASE**
PURPOSE-SPECIFIC PRODUCTS, E.G., TRANSACTIONS PROCESSING	PLATFORMS, SOFTWARE ENGINEERING, END USER COMPUTING, DISCIPLINES

Service Bureaus

MACHINE-BASED	**PEOPLE-BASED**
SERVICES PRODUCED BY MACHINES, E.G., MANUFACTURING	SERVICES PRODUCED BY PEOPLE, E.G., CUSTOMER SUPPORT, TRAINING

Audit

AUDIT
INSPECTS AND PERHAPS VETOES OTHER PEOPLE'S DECISIONS

Rainbow Analysis

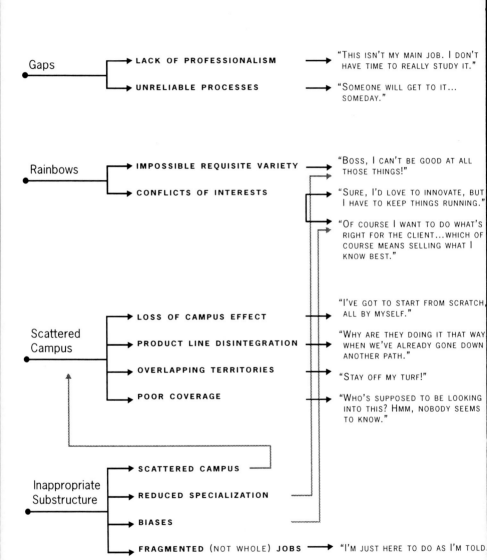

Format
of a Charter

Name of Group
CUSTOMER

CLIENTS:	PRODUCT NAME 1
	PRODUCT NAME 2
	PRODUCT NAME 3
CONSULTANTS:	PRODUCT NAME 4
	PRODUCT NAME 5
	PRODUCT NAME 6
TECHNOLOGISTS:	PRODUCT NAME 1
	PRODUCT NAME 6
	PRODUCT NAME 7
ARCHITECT:	PRODUCT NAME 1
	PRODUCT NAME 8
	PRODUCT NAME 9
PLANNING COORDINATOR:	PRODUCT NAME 1
	PRODUCT NAME 10
ORGANIZATIONAL EFFECTIVENESS:	PRODUCT NAME 1
	PRODUCT NAME 11
MACHINE-BASED SERVICE BUREAUS:	PRODUCT NAME 1
	PRODUCT NAME 7
PEOPLE-BASED SERVICE BUREAUS:	PRODUCT NAME 1
	PRODUCT NAME 12

Name of Group
SUPPLIER

CLIENTS:	PRODUCT NAME 1
	PRODUCT NAME 13
CONSULTANTS:	PRODUCT NAME 1
	PRODUCT NAME 14
	PRODUCT NAME 15
TECHNOLOGISTS:	PRODUCT NAME 1
	PRODUCT NAME 16
	PRODUCT NAME 17
ARCHITECT:	PRODUCT NAME 1
	PRODUCT NAME 18
	PRODUCT NAME 19
PLANNING COORDINATOR:	PRODUCT NAME 1
	PRODUCT NAME 19
ORGANIZATIONAL EFFECTIVENESS:	PRODUCT NAME 1
	PRODUCT NAME 20
MACHINE-BASED SERVICE BUREAUS:	PRODUCT NAME 1
	PRODUCT NAME 21
	PRODUCT NAME 22
PEOPLE-BASED SERVICE BUREAUS:	PRODUCT NAME 1
	PRODUCT NAME 23

Internal Contracts

THE BASIS OF BUSINESSLIKE RELATIONSHIPS

Figure 4

[AN INDIVIDUAL, GROUP, OR CONSORTIUM; NOT THE WHOLE COMPANY]

CUSTOMER

[THE NAME OF THE PROVIDER GROUP]

SUPPLIER

[THE NAME OF A PRODUCT FROM THE PROVIDER'S CHARTER, WITH DETAILS ATTACHED]

PRODUCT

[A COMMITMENT, NOT A WISH]

DELIVERY DATE

[THE TRUE COST TO SHAREHOLDERS, WHETHER OR NOT THE PROVIDER WILL CHARGE]

PRICE

[FIXED FEE OR TIME-AND-MATERIALS?]

TERMS

[WE CAN ONLY MEET THIS COMMITMENT IF THE CUSTOMER DOES THIS]

CUSTOMER'S ACCOUNTABILITIES

[WE CAN ONLY MEET THIS COMMITMENT IF THE WORLD DOES THIS]

RISKS AND ASSUMPTIONS

[BUDGET CENTER, DEPARTMENT NUMBER, PURSER, BLAH, BLAH, BLAH]

ADMINISTRATIVE INFORMATION

CUSTOMER   SUPPLIER

together. It incorporates the best of everyone's thinking. This not only taps their specialized knowledge, but ensures buy-in and compliance.

The Architect must be a *facilitator,* drawing on the knowledge of each of the relevant groups and building their consensus on a set of standards that will constrain their designs.

This is a small but high-level function, without a large staff but with significant potential impact. It requires a senior leader who is respected by the range of Technologists, with strong conceptual skills, broad technical knowledge, and excellent interpersonal skills.

Other Coordinators

The Architect and Planner are examples of the "Coordinators" building block -- the various types of planners -- whose purpose is *to help others with their individual responsibilities in a coordinated fashion.* Coordinators help people individually by offering expertise and methods, and at the same time help people agree with one another where consistency among peers is required. The emphasis on coordination distinguishes them from other service functions that simply help people individually and independently.

The organization may also include four other Coordinator functions (as shown in Figure 1):

* Business strategy (what business we are in) and other forms of business planning.

* Business continuity planning, including methods for disaster recovery of the Machine-based Service Bureaus, as well as for business processes recovery of clients and the organization.

* Organizational effectiveness (how we run our business, including culture, structure, internal economy, and metrics).

* Research coordination (so that everybody's research fits the plan).

Although similar in that they are coordination and facilitation functions, each of these types of Coordinators have very different backgrounds and methods, and therefore are treated as distinct structural elements.

Consultancies

In any business, customer focus is the key to long-term success. In that vein, a critical challenge facing every executive is linking the organization's work to its clients' business strategies.

To align itself with its clients' business strategies, an organization must be prepared to offer any subset of its products and services as required by its clients. But it's not easy to be business driven when you're also expected to be a proponent of a specific product line. Therefore, to build strategic alignment, organizations need a professional business-oriented *Consultancy* that is independent of any of its specific product lines -- the sales and marketing functions of the organization.

An effective Consultancy is a tremendous asset to the entire organization. Without a separate Consultancy function, the organization will continue to sell products that its clients are accustomed to buying. (In I.S., this typically means administrative data processing applications.) The Consultancy is the spearhead of strategic alignment and client partnership. As high-payoff solutions to business problems are implemented, clients will learn to perceive the organization's strategic value. This will earn the entire organization both resources and respect.

Consultants do more than act as client liaisons and "broker" projects with other groups within the organization. They also have a unique product line of their own. Consultants diagnose clients' business strategies and link mission-critical opportunities to the right subset of the organization's products and services. In this way, Consultants translate clients' strategic business opportunities into "sales" for the organization.

Consider the job requirements of the Consultancy:

* An understanding of the clients' business strategies (e.g., an M.B.A. degree and industry experience). Knowledge of the clients' organization, and the political savvy to determine which clients are most critical to strategy and, hence, most worth serving. The ability to talk to these key client executives about issues of critical concern.

* In-depth understanding of how to identify the key concerns and needs of these strategic clients; i.e., methods to diagnose high-payoff, strategic requirements (sometimes called "counselor selling").

* A broad awareness of all of the products of the organization plus a lack of technical bias, to permit purely business-driven recommendations of the solutions most appropriate to clients' needs. Any product bias whatsoever will lead to a technology-driven "solution-in-search-of-a-problem" approach.

* Excellent interpersonal skills to build healthy relations between clients and everyone in the organization.

* Behavioral skills such as interviewing, listening, mediation, and negotiation; and knowledge of participative project management methods that ensure effective organizational change.

* Knowledge of finance, decision science, economics, and policy analysis to measure value-added (strategic) benefits. This is needed to justify and evaluate solutions that generate strategic value.

* Sufficient time to spend with clients and involvement in their business so as to be readily accessible and considered part of the client's management team.

As capable as senior managers may be, they are ill equipped to do the Consultancy function. They are busy people who don't have sufficient time to spend walking the clients' halls, attending clients'

management meetings, and discussing everything from business
strategies to specific projects. Furthermore, managers are focused
on other functions, and have little time or energy to perfect the
business-driven Consulting methods of needs assessment and
benefits measurement.

The Consultancy must be separate from the Service Bureaus. The
Consultancy is focused on the implementation of new solutions -- it
must not get bogged down in day-to-day operational responsibilities.
Those who are busy fighting fires don't have time to discover new
opportunities.　　If the Consultancy were expected to operate
anything, it would find little time for new projects.

Similarly, the Consultancy should be separate from the
Technologists. The charter of the Consultancy is the converse of the
Technologists':　　Consultants are generalists in technologies and
specialists in their clients' business; Technologists are specialists in
their respective technologies, but generalists with regard to who uses
them.

To clarify this difference between Consultants and Technologists,
let's use an I.S. example.

The "Financial Applications Development" group is a Technologist
function *responsible for money-oriented applications, regardless of
which clients might need financial data.* They can build general
ledger-based applications for the United Way as easily as they can
for the company's Finance department.

The Consultant assigned to the Finance department is *responsible for
a set of clients (in Finance), regardless of what type of information
or tools they need.* The Consultant is not limited to just financial
transactions processing applications, and recommends any of the
broad range of the organization's products based on a thorough
understanding of the clients' business.

The services of the Consultancy are quite different from any offered by Technologists. Consultants and Technologists are synergistic and interdependent rather than competitive.

There are three types of Consultancies:

* **Strategic:** a small group of high-level Consultants who guarantee a stream of strategic solutions by serving key opinion-leading clients with comprehensive strategic analyses and account-management services. They are proactive, and do a lot for the few. They are analogous to a direct sales force for major accounts.

* **Retail:** a group available to anyone on demand for business advice and unbiased business diagnoses. They are reactive, and do a little for the many. They are analogous to a retail store for walk-in clients. In I.S., these are not P.C. Technologists, but rather offer the entire product line.

* **Marketing:** the one-to-many functions that promote client awareness and interpret the internal marketplace on behalf of the organization's suppliers.

The key distinction between Strategic and Retail Consultancies is in their approach to clients. Strategic Consultants proactively call on opinion leaders; Retail Consultants serve whomever calls on them. Strategic Consultants provide in-depth services for the few; Retail Consultants do a little for the many. In addition, Strategic Consultants serve as account executives, not only for the opinion leaders but also for the entire client community.

Audit

Many organizations include an Audit function, but their role is often controversial and confused.

Audit is not the same as quality inspection. In the spirit of total quality management, quality inspection is the responsibility of every producing function. It should be done every day in the normal course of doing business, not occasionally by outsiders.

Rather, Audit performs *periodic checks to ensure that people are complying with rules and policies.*

Audit involves problem identification, not problem diagnosis and repair. While Auditors may make suggestions for corrective actions based on their experience, their focus should be on examining results rather than understanding core processes.

While there are many situations that require Auditors, Audit should never be used to substitute for direction through line management. The order to comply with rules and policies must come through one's chain of command to have legitimacy, as should the directive to cooperate with Auditors. Without such legitimacy, the Auditors will have a difficult time doing their jobs, and compliance will be minimal. Auditors check on compliance; they do not replace managers by setting objectives, giving orders, or measuring results.

Audit is not only a distinct building block of structure. It must be kept entirely separate from the other service-oriented functions. It is impossible for the same people to both serve and police others, and any involvement in the Audit function compromises a group's ability to be customer-focused and to partner with those it serves. Imagine someone saying, "I'm from the Internal Revenue Service. I'd like to help you with your financial planning!" Auditors sell their services to stakeholders other than those whom they audit.

In other words, Audit should not be considered part of a service-provider organization.

PUTTING THE
PIECES TOGETHER

12. How to Design an Organization Chart

The Structural Cybernetics model makes it easy to spot organizational dysfunctions and opportunities for improvement. This can be done with an interactive process called the "Rainbow Analysis."

The first step is to identify the functions performed by each of the groups in the current organization. To do this, we assign a color to each building block, and then color code the organization chart based on what people actually do.

Once the color coding is completed, analysis can identify four types of problems (see Figure 2): gaps, rainbows, scattered campuses, and inappropriate substructures.

* **Gaps:** where a function is missing altogether, or performed part time by people whose primary focus is another function. (Look for a missing color, or for a color spread around the charts in combination with other colors.) Gaps lead to:

  - **Lack of professionalism:** with no one looking after the function as a primary effort, gaps lead to poor quality. There is no focal point for accumulating experience, and no one has time to study and evolve world-class methods.

  - **Unreliable processes:** when a function is not receiving anyone's primary attention, it is not likely to be a reliable process. Continual improvement in the process is also unlikely. For example, if no Architect is appointed, there would be no reason to expect a steady flow of decisions on standards.

* **Rainbows:**   where a group is expected to perform more than one function.   (Look for groups marked with more than one color.) Rainbows lead to two potential problems:

-   **Impossible requisite variety:**   when building blocks are combined,   the   resulting job requires a   much   greater diversity   of   skills,   exceeding most people's variety-handling   abilities.   In other words, people are expected to be experts at too many things and feel stretched too thinly. As   a   result,   they   may   be   mediocre   at   many of their assignments, and may neglect other duties altogether.

-   **Conflicts of interests:**   when people are asked to pursue conflicting   objectives,   serious   performance   problems result.   In particular, the combination of Technologists and Service   Bureaus   (invention   versus   operations),   and Technologists   and   Consultancy   (bias of the specialist versus an unbiased diagnosis of the business), lead to poor results at one of the two functions.

* **Scattered campuses:**   when a function is spread around the organization.   (Look for a color common to more than one group.) Scattered campuses raise the following concerns:

-   **Loss of the campus effect:** professional exchange among peers within a specialty is reduced, so people are less likely to learn from each other and exchange "tricks of the trade."   This slows the pace of learning and innovation, and reduces productivity.

-   **Product-line disintegration:**   it is difficult to get like experts to agree upon standards and common products. Each pocket of the profession is likely to establish its own culture,   practices,   and   standards,   so   architectural fragmentation   develops.   Also, a variety of different brands and styles of the same product may compete for the clients' attention.

- **Overlapping territories:** if no single manager is responsible for allocating domains within a function, then there is no one whose job is to ensure that every topic is covered in only one place. Expertise in a specialty may develop in one location and not be accessible to others. When it's needed elsewhere, the expertise is replicated. In time, overlaps develop, and two groups compete to deliver the same function. As a result, reinvention is common and productivity is diminished. (In I.S., opportunities for reusable code are lost.) Also, overlaps lead to territorial friction and confusion in the product line.

- **Poor coverage:** similarly, with no one manager looking after comprehensive coverage of the function, it is difficult to be sure that every topic is covered somewhere. As a result, new technologies, techniques, and services may not be researched and supported. Since there is no guarantee that the organization's product line will remain comprehensive, opportunities may be lost.

* **Inappropriate substructures:** where people are divided into groups based on something other than their specialty. Structure tells people what they are supposed to be good at. If the basis for substructure is anything other than a function's expertise, the following types of problems occur:

- Specialization will be reduced.

For example, a substructure (such as dedicating groups to clients) may be right for one function and not for another.

If the Consultancy is substructured by anything other than clients, specialization in the clients' business is reduced. Since each Consultant must cover all of the clients, the Consultants don't have as much time as they'd like with each account. Furthermore, confusion is likely. Clients have assigned to them more than one primary liaison, and have to call one person under certain conditions and another under others.

On the other hand, if Technologists are substructured by client, specialization in technologies is reduced. Each client-oriented group must cover the entire range of technologies and applications. For example, instead of having a group specializing in general ledger systems and another in tax systems, each client-oriented group must include a financial systems generalist. All of the generalists in each group must research the same topics, and develop overlapping product lines.

- Biases will be introduced.

For example, if Technologists are substructured by client and yet still expected to be specialists in a particular technology, they will be biased toward their specialty. In I.S. for example, if the group dedicated to clients in the Finance department are also specialists in general ledger systems, then it will be difficult for people in the Finance department to get anything but financial systems. It will also be difficult for anyone outside the Finance department to get needed financial systems.

- Jobs may be fragmented rather than whole.

If Technologists are substructured by tasks (e.g., planning versus doing, or development versus maintenance), jobs are not fragmented. Two groups become responsible for the same line of business, and no one will feel accountable for the product line. A poor motivational climate is likely to occur.

If Coordinator functions are divided by anything other than that which they coordinate (architecture, business plans, organizational effectiveness, research grants, business continuity), the very purpose of coordination is defeated. Processes become fragmented, synergies are lost, and integrated results are unlikely. For example, dividing the Architect function by client (or anything other than sections of the architecture) leads to disjointed and incompatible standards.

In Service Bureaus, there is a tendency to define groups by tasks rather than by the services they offer. For example, within an I.S. computer center, separate groups may do scheduling, operations, and capacity planning (all tasks), rather than manufacturing computer time, applications processing, and interactive services. This results in a lack of whole jobs -- i.e., responsibility for every aspect of a product line -- which undermines empowerment, customer focus, and entrepreneurship.

To help assemble the functional building blocks into an organization chart, the four types of problems in the Rainbow Analysis can be restated as four guidelines for the design of healthy organizations:

1. **A full-service organization includes all of the functional building blocks.** If any are missing, critical activities will not occur with reliability and quality. This does not mean that every building block must be staffed with permanent resources, whether or not demand exists. It simply means that someone must be accountable for every function, whether it be fulfilled by contractors or one's own staff. That person can then select and manage contractors, and build staff as workload warrants.

2. **A healthy structure does not combine building blocks within jobs (no rainbows).** Mixing these functional building blocks within a job definition inevitably creates impossible requisite variety and conflicts of interests that will lower performance. Thus, it is best to separate the functional building blocks (with their conflicting objectives), ideally leaving only the organization's executive responsible for more than one.

Reserving inevitable conflicts of interests for the highest possible level of the organization has a number of advantages. It ensures that the most seasoned leaders, those with the broadest strategic purview, deal with the difficult balancing acts involved in paradoxical objectives. It also separates conflicting forces so that the executive can explicitly adjust the balances amongst them.

Focusing jobs on a single functional building block also sends a clear message to everybody in the organization about their roles and their relationships to each other and to clients. Excellence comes from focusing on one subject area in great depth. Clearly focused jobs also help people understand what others in the organization offer, creating a basis for collaboration.

In a small organization, some combinations of building blocks are inevitable. When they are, combinations should be made within the same family of building blocks. It is easier to serve as a Technologist for a few different technologies than as both a Technologist and a Service Bureau.

3. **A healthy structure keeps all aspects of each building block together.** The campus of like experts (a building block) should not be scattered (either within a central organization or through decentralization), but rather should report to a common manager whose job is to ensure comprehensive and discrete coverage of the entire domain.

4. **A healthy structure use people's specialty as a basis for substructure.** The nature of each building block determines the natural basis for structure within that part of the organization.

Structural Cybernetics recommends what some would call a "functional structure." In the past few decades it has been fashionable to criticize functional structures for lacking customer focus and discouraging collaboration (i.e., building "stovepipes"). Alternatives, such as customer-aligned and matrix structures, have been tried. For the most part, these have created more problems than they've solved. The problems of poor customer focus and collaboration are real; but the structural answers that were tried were misguided.

There is no inherent reason why a functional structure cannot be customer focused. And effective coordinating mechanisms (teamwork across boundaries) can be built (or not built) in any structure.

The proper approach to building a customer-focused, team-oriented organization is to fix the root cause, not distort the structure to treat the symptoms. By fixing the root cause, leaders are free to design organization charts that eliminate redundancies and internal competition, provide people with clear focus and the chance to specialize, and minimize conflicts of interests.

The actual organizational chart which each organization develops will vary based on the range of technologies, size of the organization, span of control, stage of growth, skills, culture, and focus. Each organization must determine its own unique structure, using the functional building blocks as a precise language for design and the principles as guidelines for assembling them.

When based on principles, the organizational structure can be flatter. Empowered, self-directed groups become more feasible because the structure clarifies their lines of business. As a result, the Structural Cybernetics model, and each group's clear understanding of its charter and domain, ensures a smoothly running function with far less need for management intervention.

13. Self-managed Groups

The concept of self-managed groups may also be used as the functional building blocks are assembled into a structure. A "self-managed group" is a group of people (a structural entity) who together fulfill a function and report to a manager who otherwise would be two levels up without an intervening layer of supervision. The group as a whole acts as if there were a supervisor over them.

Self-managed groups are useful when a very small set of people represent a distinct charter and domain. This situation calls for a distinct structural entity, but perhaps the volume of work doesn't warrant a full-time manager and none of the members of the group are significantly more senior than the others. For example, in some Base Technology areas, a few "gurus" may together represent an area of technology.

Self-managed groups are also helpful when members of the group need to be placed at a higher level in the structure in order to get the grade they need to be effective (particularly in organizations where Human Resources policy does not permit people of a given grade to report to someone at the same level).

Similarly, self-managed groups may be useful when members of the group need to be placed at a higher level in the structure in order to get the political visibility that they need to be effective (particularly in status-conscious cultures). For example, a few Strategic Consultants may all report at tier one to the organization's executive (in order to attract high-level talent to this critical function), but together serve as the Consultancy "group."

Self-managed groups depend on establishing some mechanisms for sharing the duties that a supervisor would otherwise have performed. Often this takes the form of rotating responsibility for supervision among the members of the group, along with agreeing on a shared decision process. Whether by rotation or by dividing up the tasks, the group must explicitly decide how it will allocate authority and accomplish each supervisory duty.

This sharing of supervisory duties should be reinforced with some degree of shared destiny to ensure collaboration. For example, some portion of everyone's performance appraisal should be based on the performance of the whole group.

Contrary to first impressions, self-managed groups do not save head-count. Supervisory duties must be fulfilled, whether they are shared by the members of the group or concentrated in a full-time manager. The total supervisory workload may, in fact, increase as a result of the transactions costs of rotating or sharing supervisory duties.

The disadvantages of self-managed groups emanate from their inherently weaker leadership. A self-managed group may not be as coherent in its business strategy and direction, nor as strong in its representation on the management team (e.g., competing for resources and influence). A self-managed group also may be slower to agree on the acquisition of new methods and tools. Thus, new lines of business tend to get off to a slower start. In some cases, a self-managed group may be feasible only after the new structure and culture have been institutionalized.

Self-managed groups also require more attention from the manager above them, particularly if individual performance appraisals must be written. Individual coaching and career counseling are almost always required. Thus, while self-managed groups may appear to behave as a single direct report, they inevitably reduce the next level of manager's feasible span of control, and may cost an additional layer of structure elsewhere in the organization.

Self-managed groups are not a goal in themselves, although empowerment is. They are simply a convenient way of treating situations that warrant a structural separation but do not call for full-time supervision. The approach should be used with caution, however; and the proper Human Resources policies and supervisory mechanisms must be cultivated to make them work.

14. Adaptations for Small Organizations

Small organizations face all of the challenges of large organizations -- diverse client needs, demand for technical excellence, the need for integration, and expectations of operational efficiency. They just have fewer resources with which to address them.

Small organizations may mistakenly assume that the Structural Cybernetics model is too big and complex to apply to their limited headcount. This is not true! In fact, human nature and the principles of organizational cybernetics are precisely the same in large and small organizations. The Structural Cybernetics process, including the model, works well in organizations of all sizes. In smaller organizations, however, some adaptations are appropriate.

Selective outsourcing will be more prevalent in a small organization, particularly in the area of Technologists. For example, specialists in less-used and emerging technologies are hired as needed. However, someone in the organization must represent each functional building block, and be responsible for identifying and managing contractors. In the extreme, insiders may do nothing but manage contractors.

Two functions are particularly strategic and require an insider's understanding of the company. Even in the smallest organization, Coordinators and Consultancies should never be outsourced. If necessary, it is better for the organization's executive to fulfill these functions part time.

In small organizations, people may have to wear multiple "hats"; i.e., support more than one function. While this may violate the principle of requisite variety, conflicts of interests can still be eliminated.

The model provides clear guidance for combining responsibilities. Combinations should only be made *within a functional category* (i.e., vertically; for example, merging responsibility for the various

Service Bureaus) and *never across categories* (i.e., horizontally; for example, never combining Service Bureaus and Technologists).

Small- to medium-sized organizations are likely to find a very flat structure (wide span of control) appropriate. For example, all of the Strategic Consultants and a supervisor of the Retail and Marketing Consultancies might report directly to the organization's executive.

In addition to these design considerations, in smaller organizations the implementation process (summarized in Chapter 21) can be simplified since there are fewer layers of management involved.

TEAMWORK

15. Mechanisms of Teamwork

Teamwork is not a luxury; it is an essential aspect of organizational design.

Consider the fundamental reason for the existence of organizations. An organization only performs better than a collection of independent individuals if its members specialize. By specialization, each individual can become more expert at one thing. Teams of experts, of course, perform better than the independent action of a number of generalists since specialists can apply more knowledge and experience to each problem. To allow the greatest possible degree of specialization, Structural Cybernetics suggests that the functional building blocks (Service Bureaus, Technologists, Coordinators, Consultancies) be kept separate.

But specialization depends on coordination. When people specialize, no one group can stand as an island. Virtually every significant project requires a variety of talents on multi-disciplinary teams. People must cooperate. As they attempt to work together, if not well coordinated, the group of specialists will perform worse than a collection of independent generalists, since no one specialist alone can understand, much less solve, the entire problem.

Put another way, if an organization cannot form teams that combine various specialists without regard to structural boundaries, it's destined to revert into a "stovepipe" organization of self-sufficient generalists. The best-designed organization charts will have little meaning if people cannot flexibly team across organizational boundaries.

Teamwork and coordination require more than just a willingness to work together. Specific coordinating mechanisms must be designed into the organization. The organizational design must specify interdependencies so that collaboration is part of everyone's job. These interdependencies are the basis for work processes that flow naturally across organizational boundaries, combining the appropriate subset of the various functional building blocks into project teams.

Henry Mintzberg, author and professor of organizational behavior, notes a variety of alternative coordinating mechanisms: [3]

*   **Direct supervision:** where the manager takes responsibility for the work of others, instructs workers in a coordinated way, and monitors their results.

*   **Standardization of skills:** where training in a discipline or profession ensures coordination of work.

*   **Standardization of outputs:** where everyone strives for a commonly understood result; e.g., where specifications ensure that a part made by one division fits the machine made by another.

*   **Standardization of work processes:** where procedures and flow-charts coordinate activities, as on an assembly line.

*   **Mutual adjustment:** the process of lateral communication and coordination; i.e., the "network organization" (described in the next Chapter).

Direct Supervision

The traditional approach to coordinating people's activities depends on a hierarchy of managers to coordinate work. *Direct supervision* is based on the assumption that people will only work together if their boss tells them to.

Direct supervision is a simple approach to teamwork. People who need to work together are put under a common boss. Managers form project teams comprised of people who report to them, assign work, direct their activities, and coordinate results. When people in different parts of the company have to work together, commitments are made by the boss they have in common (or special deals are

made by bosses of sufficient level), and disputes are raised through
the layers of the hierarchy until a common boss is found.

While direct supervision is indeed the most widely practiced
approach to coordination, under recent pressures hierarchy is
breaking down. The growth of business pace and complexity has
taxed the limits of management's abilities. Expecting top
management to form project teams, direct people's activities, make
decisions, and resolve disputes is unrealistic. Managers cannot
understand every nuance of myriad, complex multi-disciplinary
processes. In the face of exploding variety, management has lost its
ability to keep up, and as a result has become a bottleneck
constraining the responsiveness and flexibility of the entire
organization. As a result, traditional organizations cannot respond
fast enough to their rapidly changing environments.

Meanwhile, depending on the hierarchy of managers disempowers
people throughout the organization and wastes their talents. Recent
attention to *"empowerment"* is a rational response to the bottlenecks
created when direct supervision is used as a coordinating
mechanism. Empowerment means dismantling hierarchy as a
coordinating mechanism. However, if hierarchical coordination is
not explicitly replaced by some other coordinating mechanism, the
organization will deteriorate into chaos and paralysis. Since
management will not let that happen, many well-intentioned
empowerment programs fail as management steps back in and
retakes control to avoid disaster. True empowerment depends on
breaking away from the "boss" as the leader of every project, and
depends on building another type of coordinating mechanism.

Standardization of Skills

For *standardization of skills* to work as a coordinating mechanism,
each member of a multi-disciplinary project team must understand
the skills and activities of every other member of the team well
enough to anticipate their actions and adapt to them. One common
example is the hospital operating room, where a surgeon, an
anesthesiologist, and a nurse can work well together even though

they do not share a common boss. Another is the crew of an airplane, where the pilot, co-pilot, navigator, and flight attendants work together although they may not know each other or work for the same boss. In each of these cases, people essentially do the same things day after day, so that their actions can be anticipated just by knowing a little about the position they hold and their profession.

As well as it works in some settings, standardization of skills has limited applicability to management and professional work. Managers and professionals do not do the same thing day after day, and their actions cannot be anticipated simply by being aware of their skills and job titles. One professional cannot anticipate the practices and decisions of another to a sufficient degree to ensure effective teamwork simply by knowing the other's specialty.

Standardization of Outputs

Standardization of outputs means specifying the interface between the work of two groups so precisely that they do not need to coordinate their work any further. For example, when an automobile manufacturer orders sub-assemblies from its suppliers, very clear specifications are provided. Thereafter, they need only coordinate quantities and schedules, not details of the work.

Standardization of outputs works very well in mass production situations. However, for custom work such as that of managers and professionals, establishing clear specifications *is* the coordination that must be accomplished through some mechanism, again and again, for each new project. Standardization of outputs only applies to copies of the work, not to the collaboration required to initially produce the specifications. It is of little value when most of the work is customized, as in the case of professional work.

Standardization of Work Processes

Standardization of work processes coordinates work through a predefined procedure. This is the essence of business process reengineering (B.P.R.).

However, most business activities cannot be structured into an assembly line (or even a few assembly lines). It is impossible to predict in advance the precise combination of skills and sequence of events that will be required to deliver a customized product, as might be done in a procedures manual or work-flow diagram. The process-reengineered function may be very efficient at what it did in the past because it minimizes the need for collaboration across organizational boundaries on traditional projects. But it is ill equipped to handle the variety of today's dynamic business environment.

The challenge facing a professional organization is complex: it must quickly form unique teams of specialists suited to the unique requirements of each project -- not the same set of people for every project. Exacerbating the complexity is the fact that each individual may be a member of multiple project teams and participate in a variety of work flows. And each project team must design processes appropriate to the project at hand -- not the same process for every project. Creative and flexible process design is required, even in the most routine operational areas.

As a coordinating mechanism, all three forms of standardization are only appropriate in stable environments with predictable, well-structured relationships and processes. While these approaches are relatively simple, they cannot handle the complex and volatile reality faced by most professional organizations.

3.   Mintzberg, Henry. *Structure in Fives: Designing Effective Organizations.* Englewood Cliffs, NJ: Prentice-Hall. 1983. Page 4.

16. The Network Organization

Rather than depend on direct supervision or standardization for coordination, Structural Cybernetics builds the *"network organization"* -- a form of mutual adjustment where collaboration flows laterally across the organization. It establishes a mechanism for flexibly defining team members and processes within each project, rather than always following one predefined work flow.

In the network organization, the purpose of structure is to create well-defined loci of expertise -- not to minimize the need for collaboration (e.g., minimize hand-offs). The experts within these "entrepreneurships" are then *flexibly and dynamically combined into project teams that comprise the right skills for each project.*

As projects arise (or services are delivered), teams are formed without need for management intervention. Explicit methods then help team members determine a *flow of work (and accountability) within the team optimized to the unique nature of the project.* As a result, each team combines the right mix of specialists -- across organizational boundaries -- and manages its own tasks.

In practical terms, every entrepreneur is responsible for arranging the necessary resources for each of his or her projects. How does this work? Each group considers all the other groups (within the organization and throughout the company) as potential customers and suppliers. Whenever any group makes a commitment to a client, it becomes a "prime contractor." The prime contractor then "hires" subcontractors, who "sell" to the prime contractor either their time or specific deliverables. People have an incentive to draw others onto their project teams because entrepreneurs are more competitive when they utilize the services of specialized sub-contractors rather than attempt to do everything themselves. And people have an incentive to help each other since internal customers are customers nonetheless, and it's important to please them.

Since everyone who takes on a project is responsible for identifying his or her subcontractors, teams are assembled without having to wait for management to get involved. In other words, teams are spontaneously *self-forming*. Through this *network* of contractors and subcontractors, lateral collaboration, i.e., teamwork replaces the hierarchy or standardization as a means of coordinating work.

The concept of "internal customer-supplier relationships" is essential to make the network organization work. As sensible as this perspective is, for many people, a significant paradigm shift is required before they view peers within the organization as customers.

Such a cultural change does not occur by simply redesigning the organization chart and establishing new cultural principles. More explicit and tangible mechanisms are needed to ensure that the right people are on each project team. In Structural Cybernetics, this is addressed through *"charters."*

As a business within a business, every group in the organization needs to have a clear understanding not only of its products but also of its internal customers and suppliers. To build the necessary skills and habits, each entrepreneurship develops a list of types of people throughout the company with which it does business. In Structural Cybernetics, this is called a "charter." (See Figure 3.)

A charter is not a mission statement. Rather, it is comprised of two lists: the group's customers (both clients and others within the organization) and the products it "sells" to each; and the group's suppliers and the products it "buys" from each.

In charters, the word "product" refers to both products and services. Each product is defined in terms of its *deliverables,* not the tasks required to produce it.

Charters are rich and flexible descriptions of all the many work flows and subcontracting relationships, and have very positive effects on teamwork. They define boundaries to prevent territorial disputes, and specify interdependencies to encourage teaming. Charters weave collaboration into the fabric of the organization.

Charters also have a powerful impact on an organization's culture by clarifying what business each group is in and reinforce an entrepreneurial spirit. This produces a number of positive effects. Defining jobs in terms of results is the basis for *empowerment.* Each group is evaluated based on its ability to deliver the products in its charter, without management attempting to control the tasks it performs to produce those results. The product focus also brings *awareness of competition.* Charters also build a *customer-focused culture,* since everyone must understand exactly what his or her group sells to each of its customers.

The supplier side of the charter is the basis for *self-forming teams.* It encourages people to "buy" from each other rather than make for themselves, which discourages replication of skills and facilities. And by telling people where to go for each type of help they might need, the supplier side of the charter guides everyone in forming teams without management intervention. Collaboration automatically ripples through the entire organization, as each subcontractor in turn identifies his or her own suppliers.

The supplier side of the charter also ensures a *clear flow of accountability* within each project team. Instead of vague roles and responsibilities, one member of the project team is designated the "prime contractor." All others are subcontractors accountable for specific deliverables within the broader project, that is, for specific products sold to the prime contractor.

Charters can also help managers measure results. Performance appraisals can be based not only on the opinion of one's supervisor, but also on the satisfaction of a well-defined list of internal customers, and the assessment of one's teamwork and project management skills by team members and suppliers.

In total, writing charters helps each entrepreneur build a sense of *ownership* of a piece of the organization's business. This supports an entrepreneurial attitude and fosters a high level of commitment.

17. The Businesslike Practice of Contracting

Even if the organization chart and charters are well designed, people will have to learn to trust each other before they'll depend on teamwork.

In the past, people felt that they had to "own the bodies" to be sure necessary work was done, often because they felt they couldn't trust other groups to satisfy their needs. This isolationism led to a replication of expertise, which forced each group to become a "jack of all trades." Such reduction in specialization damaged the performance of everyone in the entire organization, and led to overlapping territories, internal competition, and a politically-charged atmosphere that discouraged teamwork.

Even with a preference for self-sufficiency, at some point managers invariably find themselves depending on peers. Unfortunately, if internal commitments are not clear, collaboration is often problematic. How much time does the typical manager spend sorting out misunderstandings between clients and staff, and clarifying their mutual roles and accountabilities for projects and services? Most would say, "Too much!"

The network organization absolutely depends on effective teamwork. In it, people work with their peers in other groups rather than replicate their expertise. People need not have the necessary skills *reporting* to them. Instead, they "buy" help from the appropriate peer group. Entrepreneurs would rather "buy than make" because, as a customer, they get all the benefits of control over others' results without the headaches of managing people.

Effective teamwork (a willingness to buy from each other) is not simply a matter of friendly relationships. Working together well requires business practices that are conducive to mutual trust. The network organization creates an atmosphere of trust through *"contracts."* As people within the organization interact with their customers (both clients and each other), they make commitments --

i.e., form contracts -- to deliver products and services. These contracts clarify people's mutual accountabilities.

By contract, we do not mean an extensive legal tome. Also, we do not mean to imply that money changes hands; this is a matter of the internal economy, not structure. A contract is a simple statement, either verbal or written, which documents a mutual understanding. It is comprised of the following basic elements (see Figure 4):

* The customer's name.
* The supplier's name.
* The product and key deliverables.
* The delivery date.
* The price and terms.
* The customer's accountabilities.
* The risks and assumptions outside the supplier's control.
* Any necessary administrative information.
* Signatures (when appropriate).

Through contracting, the network organization avoids the problems resulting from unclear accountability that plague many teams. Instead of everyone attempting to look after the whole project (making roles and accountability unclear), a prime contractor is accountable to the client to deliver the end result, and serves as a project manager and systems integrator at the highest level. While all strive to please the client, subcontractors are ultimately accountable to the prime contractor, not the client. Of course, the prime contractor is very interested in the subcontractors' ideas, since they might help please the client. With this clear flow of accountability, everyone understands who is in control (and hence accountable for total results). "Finger pointing" and battles for control disappear, and teamwork is enhanced.

18. Flexible Teaming

The network organization is extremely flexible -- far more so than other types of coordinating mechanisms. Unlike business process reengineering, the network organization is not limited to a few predefined work flows which may or may not fit the needs of the project. Each project leader can arrange whatever teams and work flows are warranted by the particular project. Project plans are automatically tailored to fit the unique requirements of each situation, as work flows along a unique path through the network of experts in the organization. As a result, processes are defined in a dynamic, purpose-driven way.

Throughout each of these processes, Consultants, Technologists, Coordinators, and Service Bureaus are all involved at various points in each project. It is unnecessarily limiting to define relationships in terms of "hand-offs," where one group turns a project over to another at a certain point in time to carry forward. Instead, each group contributes its unique value (i.e., "sells" its unique product line) at the appropriate point in the process.

Traditionally, people have viewed organizational work flows as sequential processes. For example, the organization first develops a strategic plan, then makes any necessary architectural decisions, then prioritizes the projects within the plan, and finally implements those projects. This philosophy leads to a slow-moving organization that has difficulty responding to changes in business strategy or technologies between planning cycles.

Instead, we view organizations as a set of *parallel, linked dynamic systems* which together produce the organization's products.

Since all of these processes are ongoing and independent, they can all be as responsive as necessary. Their tempo need not be the same. For example, a project can be pursued whenever the need arises, without necessarily awaiting a planning process. And because these processes are interlinked, the entire organizational system remains integrated and synchronized.

Thinking in terms of parallel, linked dynamic systems requires a mental shift -- like the change from programming conventional computer systems to designing software for massively parallel processors. This new perspective, rooted in cybernetics, is fundamental to designing responsive, flexible, entrepreneurial organizations.

FADS, FALLACIES,
AND COMMON SENSE

19. Sensible Outsourcing

Many organizations are interested in outsourcing -- that is, paying other firms to perform all or part of their work. In some cases, interest originates with top executives who use outsourcing as a threat to force change.

Outsourcing vendors have promised dramatic savings, along with enhanced flexibility and the vision that line executives will have more time to focus on their core businesses. While on the surface these   claims   seem plausible, they do not hold up well under scrutiny.

Claims versus Reality

Consider the following claimed benefits of outsourcing and the reality underlying each:

*   **Reduced costs.**

   Claim: Economies of scale will reduce costs.

   Reality: The outsourcing vendor must earn a profit at the customer's expense.   Furthermore, external contracting brings added sales and transactions costs.

   The   only lasting cost savings occur where there are true economies of scale *across corporate boundaries*. One common example is long-distance telecommunications. There are other cases where inter-organizational sharing is possible, but such cases   must be examined carefully.   For example in I.S., hardware   no longer shows economies of scale, and many software licenses are corporation specific.

*   **Increased flexibility.**

Claim: Outsourcing converts fixed costs (or relatively fixed costs such as people) into variable costs, giving the firm greater financial flexibility.

Reality: Most outsourcing vendors require long-term contracts that provide them with stable revenues over time. Renegotiating these contracts may be more expensive than changing internal commitments. If flexibility is the goal, the contract must be carefully negotiated to allow variability in demand and cost. Generally, demanding this flexibility comes at a relatively high price.

*   **Downsizing.**

Claim: In organizations that must downsize, the outsourcing vendor will move surplus people to other jobs serving other companies. This appears more humanistic, since people may not be laid off.

Reality: If those other jobs exist, surplus staff can compete for them on the open market with or without the outsourcing deal. If they are good enough to deserve those other positions, they will get them -- whether or not the organization pursues outsourcing. On the other hand, if they are not good enough to win other jobs on their own merits, it is unlikely that the highly competitive outsourcing vendors will keep them in these positions for long. Thus, ultimately, outsourcing does little to change the employment picture for surplus people.

*   **Better access to technology.**

Claim: Equipment vendors suggest that outsourcing through them provides customers with better access to new technologies.

Reality: Vendor sales representatives are eager to bring new products to their customers' attention, with or without an outsourcing relationship. And it is always better to decide on one's own to adopt a new vendor offering than to leave it up to the vendor (who has an obvious vested interest in selling every new product). Meanwhile, vendor-owned outsourcing services are less likely to tap opportunities presented by competitive vendors (e.g., more cost-effective, "plug-compatible" products).

* **Stick to the knitting.**

Claim: Outsourcing leaves business managers more time to focus on the company's main lines of business.

Reality: This is only true if the people who used to manage the outsourced function are transferred into other business functions. On the other hand, if these managers are fired or transferred to the outsourcing vendor, there will be no greater number of business managers left focusing on the "knitting" than there were before outsourcing. In other words, the business only gets more attention if line-management headcount is expanded (and costs are increased). Of course, line-management headcount can be expanded with or without outsourcing a staff function.

* **Less management distraction.**

Claim: Outsourcing relieves top management of having to worry about managing another staff function.

Reality: Managing an outsourcing vendor is no easier (and often more difficult) than managing an internal staff executive. Contracts and legal interpretations are involved, and it's not always easy to guide people when you don't write their performance appraisals.

If top management does indeed become less involved in managing a staff function such as I.S., outsourcing may be counterproductive. Those who understand the strategic value of I.S. argue that management should spend more, not less, time thinking about it. Without management involvement, there is danger that the I.S. function will do little more than it has done in the past. That is, it may continue to invest in administrative systems, but will find few breakthroughs in strategic applications. This tendency to stick to past activities and miss new strategic opportunities is exacerbated by the extra fees associated with doing anything beyond the originally-contracted workload.

*   **Greater competence.**

Claim: Outsourcing vendors are more experienced and competent than internal staff.

Reality: An organization can hire competent managers as readily as an outsourcing vendor.

*   **Cash flow.**

Claim: Outsourcing is a source of near-term cash, since assets may be sold to the outsourcing vendor.

Reality: Selling a strategic resource is a drastic way to save a sinking firm. Since selling a critical staff function risks crippling all remaining business units and increasing long-term costs, it might be better to sell a line business unit and leave the remaining businesses in a healthier position.

*   **Pain killer.**

Claim: In some cases, outsourcing is simply a matter of paying someone else to experience the pain of managing a dysfunctional department rather than expending the energy to think through how to make that function healthy again.

Reality: This costly escapism sacrifices a valuable component of business strategy for a short-term convenience.

A Sensible Approach to Outsourcing

Upon scrutiny, outsourcing an entire staff function often fails to live up to its promises, and carries with it numerous risks. It generally increases costs, reduces flexibility, and constrains strategic value. Thus, after investigation, many firms have shied away from outsourcing all or major portions of a staff function.

Nonetheless, external consultants and contractors do bring skills and abilities that can complement internal staff. Thus, many firms are pursuing a selective outsourcing strategy. Indeed, the use of contractors and consultants, which is not new, is a healthy form of outsourcing.

To sort out jobs appropriate for outsourcers from those best kept inside, we must first understand the unique advantages of the internal staff. There are two key reasons why insiders have an advantage over outsourcing vendors: continuity and vested interests.

Continuity: Internal staff have a history with the organization that provides them with a better understanding of the clients' culture, strategies, and politics. And with the expectation of continuity, people know they'll be around to deal with the consequences of their actions. This results in improved partnerships, which pay off in both greater client satisfaction and improved strategic alignment.

On the other hand, outsourcing vendors may rotate their staff more frequently, and their people develop loyalties to the outsourcing vendor rather than to the organization.

Vested interests: Outsourcing vendors may be sincere about partnership, but ultimately they work for different shareholders and ethically must (and will) place their shareholders' interests first.

For example, in a needs-assessment interview with a client, what would happen if the I.S. Consultant sees an opportunity for either a $200,000 administrative application which could save clerical time, or a $200 end user computing tool which could significantly impact the client's personal effectiveness at delivering the company's strategy?   While the latter may provide far higher payoff and more strategic value, the outsourcing vendor has a strong incentive to recommend the more lucrative administrative project since it generates more revenues (costs to the organization).

For both these reasons, insiders are more likely to be invited to partner with clients, and will be in a better position to contribute to the strategic imperatives of the firm.

So long as the right tasks are kept for insiders -- those where an insiders' advantage (continuity and appropriate vested interests) are important -- outsourcing selected activities can be quite valuable.

The goals of selective outsourcing include the following:

*   Minimize fluctuations in headcount that could result from peaks and valleys in demand.

*   Maximize development of employees by outsourcing less interesting or end-of-life work.

*   Minimize costs by utilizing relatively less expensive employees whenever possible, or sharing costs with other corporations.

External "consultants," who are hired to transfer their skills and methods and improve employees' effectiveness, should be managed differently from "contractors," who do work in place of employees. Ideally, each is used as follows:

*   Consultants may be used by anyone whenever justifiable.

*   Contractors should be used when economies of scale across corporate boundaries produce true cost savings. They may also be used to off-load commodity work from internal staff, or to handle peak loads. Contractors should never be used to perform new, growth-oriented activities while internal staff are left with obsolescent work.

Managing Outsourcing Vendors:
The Open Organization

For all practical purposes, outside contractors relate to people --
clients and other groups in the organization -- just as their inside
counterparts do.   The fact that their paycheck is written by a
different corporation does not change the nature of their work or
their relationships with others on project teams.

This leads to a key guideline: *Outsourcers should be treated as part
of the internal group that offers the same skills and products.*

We term this concept the *open organization.*   From the internal
entrepreneur's   point   of   view, every vendor and outsourcing
contractor   is   considered part of one's group.   Each internal
entrepreneur should cultivate contacts with outside contractors and
vendors in its area of expertise, and then manage them as part of its
staff.   And each internal entrepreneur should proactively decide
whether to "make or buy" in the course of every project.

One   advantage   to   this   approach   is that it clearly assigns
responsibility for acquiring and managing outsourcers. The people
best qualified to select contractors, manage them, and judge their
work are those in the same profession. Every entrepreneur must
develop a network of external counterparts to help with peak loads
and fill in gaps in skills.

Another advantage of the open organization is that all outsourcing
vendors will automatically live within the structural model and its
charters and domains.   This insulates clients from the distinction
between internal and external resources; and they need not worry
about who is chosen to staff their projects.

By   bringing   contractors   into   the   organization through the
appropriate internal group, competition is avoided.   Of course,
clients have the right to go elsewhere if an internal staff function is

not competitive. But there are far less expensive and less risky ways to keep internal entrepreneurs "honest," such as benchmarking and performance management.

Treating contractors as extensions to internal entrepreneurships also allows the internal professionals to ensure architectural compliance and quality. Furthermore, new skills and technologies can be transferred to internal staff in the process of working with contractors. This gives clients a point of contact for ongoing support after the project is completed and the contractors are gone.

Even when outsourcers do most of the work, internal staff add value in a number of ways. Specifically, they are responsible for four functions:

* Generating entrepreneurial ideas within one's charter and domain, and deciding whether to "make or buy."

* Shopping for the best deal, negotiating the contract, and managing contractor performance.

* Resolving any problems in the relationship, and maintaining a healthy collaboration between the two companies.

* Establishing clear internal contracts with customers and suppliers, and retaining responsibility for fulfilling those contracts (whether outsourcing vendors are involved or not).

Indeed, people should be proactive in using contractors. In the interest of offering their customers the best possible deal and maintaining one's preferred-vendor status, internal entrepreneurs should be the first to offer contractors or commercial packages.

And whenever peaks in demand warrant, entrepreneurs should acquire resources (funded by their clients) rather than lose the business. This way, they are never resource constrained. The only constraint on an entrepreneurship's capabilities is its customers' ability to pay for the work they need. The alternative -- asking clients to work directly with outside contractors -- not only puts a greater burden on the client, but also builds the habit of buying elsewhere which leads to permanent losses of market share.

Smart entrepreneurs would rather buy than make. Through the concept of the open organization, clients get the best of both the internal staff and outsourcing.

20. The Trade-offs of Decentralization

Many people believe that decentralization will improve the responsiveness and value of a staff function. On the other hand, decentralization has often led to disappointments: less innovation, fragmented work, ruined career paths, and lower quality. And costs rise, sometimes by as much as 50 percent.

Some organizations have experienced a painful and expensive "pendulum swing" between centralization and decentralization. Part of the reason for this is the structure of the organization.

For example, if Consultancy and Technologists jobs are combined, we may decentralize both in order to become more responsive to the unique mission-critical needs of the clients -- that is, to do a better job of Consultancy. In doing so, we lose control of architecture and our ability to specialize as Technologists.

Pressures then build for recentralization of the Technologist function that should never have been fragmented, and with the next reorganization the company centralizes both that which should be central (Technologists) and that which perhaps should remain decentralized (Consultancy). The result is pendulum-like structural change -- alternately centralizing and decentralizing a function. Each reorganization is a backlash to the other, demonstrating that neither the extremes nor the middle work.

The pendulum swing occurs when organizational changes lack resolution -- that is, when decentralization or recentralization is applied across the board to a range of structural building blocks, rather than adjusting the degree of decentralization for each function independently. In the above example, the cycle can be broken by separating the Consultancy and Technologist functions and adjusting the degree of decentralization separately for each.

To analyze the trade-offs, a precise definition of "decentralization" is necessary. Decentralization does not refer to geographic dispersion.   People can be placed anywhere in the world, and yet still report to a central organization.

Specifically, decentralization means two things: substructuring a function by client (rather than by skill or product, for example); and moving lines of reporting to clients (rather than a single companywide functional executive).

The key to understanding decentralization is in the first half of the definition: Decentralization necessarily substructures a function by client.   If this is appropriate, then decentralization can work (provided other mechanisms are implemented to coordinate similar professionals).   On the other hand, if substructuring by client is inappropriate for the function, dysfunctions are inevitable.

Since the basis for substructure should match the nature of people's expertise, the only functional building block amenable to decentralization is Consultancy, the function whose specialty is knowing the clients.   When any of the other building blocks are substructured by client, the degree of specialization is reduced. When Technologists are decentralized, for example, clients will find themselves with small groups of generalists trying to keep up with the rapid pace of technological change throughout the entire discipline.   Since they cannot possibly stay current as well as specialists can, their productivity drops, it takes them longer to produce work, quality suffers, innovation slows, and costs rise.

Furthermore, decentralization scatters the campus of similar experts. In the case of Technologists, this leads to redundant research efforts, reinvention, and fragmented results.   In Service Bureaus, economies of scale are lost.   And, of course, career paths suffer since young people are not mentored by specialists in their field, and have few opportunities for promotion within their profession.   Again, one visible result is higher costs.

But what about the advantages of decentralization? Many of the claimed benefits are questionable:

* **Understanding of the business.**

    Claim: By reporting to the business, staff people will better understand business strategies.

    Reality: It's true that substructuring people by client focuses them on knowing their clients while they become generalists with regard to technologies and professional methods. This is appropriate for Consultants, and inappropriate for all other building blocks.

* **Tailoring to unique local needs.**

    Claim: People who report to a business unit will be more likely to tailor solutions to the unique needs of that business unit.

    Reality: Centralization does not imply that "one size fits all." There is no reason a central group cannot sell individual clients solutions tailored to their unique needs, while still taking advantage of some portion of the work they have done for others.

* **Client control over priorities.**

    Claim: Clients can control the priorities of people who report to them more easily than those of centralized staff groups.

    Reality: You don't need to own your own grocery store to control what you eat. Similarly, clients can own spending power and control the priorities of a central staff organization without managing the headcount. In this case, the answer is found in a healthy internal economy, not structure.

*   **Access to client executives.**

Claim: Decentralized staff will have better access to business executives than centralized staff.

Reality: A staff person reporting a few levels below a business-unit executive may, in fact, not have better access to executives than a peer in a corporate staff function. Often, local politics prevent insiders from attending executive meetings where people who are outside the clients' hierarchy may be welcome.

*   **Customer focus.**

Claim: Reporting to the business unit will make people more customer focused.

Reality: If a group is unresponsive and bureaucratic, decentralizing it only creates many little unresponsive bureaucracies.   On the other hand, there is no reason why a centralized group cannot learn a customer-focused culture.

Even in Consultancy, the advantages of decentralization are questionable. Decentralized Consultants' efforts are often diluted as they are assigned other projects, or expand their scope and become minature full-service organizations.   Partnerships deteriorate when decentralized Consultants see their job as defending their clients against the centralized organization, or attempt to speak on behalf of clients and fulfill clients' responsibilities. Decentralized Consultants rarely collaborate to perfect their methods. Furthermore, opportunities for multi-client consortia (cross-functional projects) are lost.

Decentralization is a costly way to treat organizational problems. A better answer is to address the root cause of the problems by building a healthy central organization.   In fact, most of the pressures for decentralization disappear if the organization has an effective Consultancy, a healthy internal economy that gives clients control over priorities, a customer-focused culture, and effective entrepreneurs that take advantage of their consolidation and specialize as much as possible to better serve their customers.

IDEAS TO ACTION

21. Implementing Structural Change

Every organization is unique. That's why each organization's structure must be tailored to its unique culture, workload, and people.

And that's why the Structural Cybernetics model is not an "ideal" organizational chart prescribed verbatim for any company. Rather, it is a functional description of the various activities performed by an organization -- the building blocks of structure -- and a set of principles that explains how these activities are interrelated. Structural Cybernetics is an analytical tool that can identify needed changes in an organization's structure and processes. Its purpose is to help each organization assemble the building blocks into a unique structure appropriate for its unique needs.

A well-designed structure has an extremely powerful impact on people. It can bring about significant paradigm shifts and dramatic cultural change. But achieving such a transformation requires more than just good design; the way the new organization is implemented is equally important.

Just announcing a new organization chart achieves very little. When new organizational structures are *mandated* top down by senior executives, the results are unsatisfactory for four main reasons:

* Mandated structures don't reflect a *depth of knowledge* of "the way things really work around here." The design process requires a detailed understanding of the current functions, needs of the business, and day-to-day activities that must be represented in the structural design -- a level of detail held only by the broader cross-section of people who work within the organization. Their input is absolutely critical to successful structural design.

* Mandating a new structure does little to help people at all levels of the organization *understand the spirit of their new roles.*

Without such an understanding of assigned entrepreneurships, it is unreasonable to expect them to evolve toward excellence.

*   Mandated structures do little to *change the way an organization actually does business,* i.e., its processes and culture. For structural change to bring about meaningful cultural change, the design and implementation process must educate people in a new way of doing business. People must learn new relationships with others, both within and outside the organization, and new modes of operation that engender high-performance teamwork.

This sort of cultural change is not just "nice to have." Effective structure *depends* on cultural change. The separation of the building blocks requires effective collaboration, since no one function alone can produce the organization's products. However, if people in the organization can't work well with one another, then each small group must fulfill all the functions on its own, and the organization will slip back into isolated islands of self-sufficient generalists.

People must learn to collaborate well across boundaries to make the organizational system as a whole work. To build effective teamwork, people must view the organization as an interdependent set of dynamic systems, and learn new processes of teamwork.

*   It is difficult to obtain *commitment* to a mandated structure. As in any significant change, the support of the people who must make it work is critical. Their commitment is built through the sense of ownership that results from meaningful participation in the design of the new structure.

For all of these reasons, working out the appropriate structure is not a job for the organization's executive alone. Even if the organization's executive could design the ideal structure, simply announcing a new organization chart has limited impact. It may clarify territories, but a chart alone will not build a customer-focused, entrepreneurial, team-oriented culture.

Therefore, a *participative* process of structural change is essential. The design and implementation process must involve the people who will be affected by the change, to take advantage of their knowledge and build their understanding and commitment. Like a barn raising, the community works together to design and implement the kind of organization in which people want to work.

Participative structural design can be a delicate process. People's careers and quality of work life are at stake. Structural changes can be politically and emotionally difficult for all involved. And participation can deteriorate into a "free for all" based on political clout, personality issues, or individual career problems -- undermining the logic and viability of the structure.

Two sets of agreements are the basis of healthy participation: a clear, common *language* of structure, and objective *principles* of design. These agreements help participants communicate in unambiguous terms, and guide them to apply their in-depth knowledge of the workings of the organization in a rational manner rather than just lobby for personal gain.

In this way, Structural Cybernetics provides a systematic basis for participative design, facilitating healthy contributions from everyone while avoiding political contests. It is *not an "off-the-shelf" design* that applies to any and all organizations. In fact, it is just the opposite. It allows those who must live within the organization to design it, and in the process, understand it as a dynamic system. In a series of carefully orchestrated workshops, people not only create a new organization chart, but they also design a new culture and a new way of doing business.

Healthy contributions depend on people being open and objective. This is unlikely if people are worried about protecting their jobs or their "turf." Some guarantees are necessary to build a safe environment conducive to open participation, and to elicit the maximum commitment to the new organization. Generally, guarantees to participants include the following:

* No one will lose compensation as a result of restructuring.

* No one will lose their job as a result of restructuring. Any necessary headcount reductions should occur before (or well after) structural change. If job losses are blamed on the new structure, the new organization will be resented and not seen as a positive change leading to a healthy work environment for those who remain.

* No one will be forced to relocate as a result of restructuring.

The Structural Cybernetics implementation process employs a "cascade" strategy. Initially, participants include all candidates for tier-one positions (i.e., those who might report directly to the organization's executive). The facilitators teach participants the language and principles of Structural Cybernetics, and then allow participants a forum for testing and adapting it. People use the model to diagnose existing problems, and then to design a new structure.

Then, actual tier-one leaders are selected from the candidate pool that designed the new structure. Their involvement in design ensures a deep understanding of and commitment to the new organization. Selected tier-one leaders then work on the teamwork processes which will tie together their various entrepreneurships.

With a solid understanding at tier one of how the new organization will work, the process cascades to tier two. In this phase, the tier-one leaders become the teaching team, and the tier-two candidates are involved in the design of tier-two structure. Once tier-two leaders are selected, they too study how processes will work in the new organization.

Participation is not limited to top management. Care is taken to communicate   clearly to employees and to clients who are not directly involved in the process. To ensure this, a communication plan is carefully crafted at every step of the process.

Finally,   all   tier-one and tier-two leaders together become the teaching   team,   and   the   process cascades to the rest of the organization.   This roll-out and migration process is carefully orchestrated to ensure effective and lasting change at every level of the organization with a minimum of disruption and risk.

Throughout this process, the Human Resources function assists with job design and evaluation, career tracking, and recruiting.

This participative process requires significant effort, but pays off in an   organization   that   is different in powerful ways: People throughout the organization feel empowered as entrepreneurs. They treat clients in a business-like manner, and treat each other as customers and suppliers. The result is an unbeatable combination of specialization, teamwork, and customer focus.

And thanks to the time spent planning, the new organization "hits the   ground   running,"   with widespread understanding of and commitment to new ways of doing business. Cultural change is accomplished at the same time as structural change.

The results of such an investment are enduring. So long as leaders remain committed to the vision, a principles-based organizational structure can last a lifetime, evolving gracefully over time rather than periodically demanding radical changes. As new business problems arise, the staff within the organization will implicitly know their respective roles in solving them. Similarly, adjustments to the clients'   organizational   structure,   business strategies, new technologies, or the degree of decentralization can be made without significant   reorganizations.   With an organization that adapts flexibly within consistent, stable principles, one no longer needs to hear that plaintive cry, "What, another reorganization!?"

22. The Role of the Systematic Executive

As the business world becomes more complex and fast paced, it's all too easy for an executive to become a bottleneck. Rather than design products or make day-to-day decisions, the executive's job is to design a healthy work environment so that the whole organization delivers its product line effectively, day after day, with or without the executive's involvement. In other words, the job of the systematic executive is to design an organization in which everyone can succeed.

Building a healthy organization is by far the most important and pressing responsibility facing today's executive. And it is a highly leveraged use of the executive's time. By setting up an environment that sends the right signals, and then empowering and coaching people throughout the organization, the executive's vision can be translated into action many times over.

Structure is not a panacea, but it is one of the most powerful tools of leadership, and fundamental to an organization's success.

Of the five basic dimensions of organizational design (culture, structure, internal economy, methods and skills, metrics and rewards), structure is generally the right place to start a process of systemic change to build a high-performance organization. People cannot succeed at fundamentally unhealthy jobs, no matter how smart and willing they may be. It is the responsibility of executives to correct performance problems by fixing root causes, not symptoms, i.e., the structure of the organization.

Structural Cybernetics can bring about ambitious transformational change in a safe, well-planned, and well-tested process. But the executive's work is never done. Once a healthy organizational structure is in place, the executive must continually reinforce it. Continual nurturing and evolution requires time and thought, and at times may demand difficult decisions. But this is a high-payoff use of an executive's time, and a duty that brings great rewards: the joy of seeing people blossom and the organization succeed.

The systematic executive is neither a technocrat nor a general business manager without experience in the organization's business. The job requires a specialist -- not in the organization's technologies, but in its leadership -- a leader combines business and functional knowledge with a deep understanding of the science of organizational health.

Afterword

Currently, most organizations are socially rather than technically constrained. In such cases, a high-performance organization typically does not depend on acquiring new technologies or resources, but rather on building more effective working relationships and methods.

Numerous executives have used Structural Cybernetics to bring significant change to a variety of I.S. (and other staff) organizations. As we worked with them, NDMA refined the implementation process in order to maximize people's buy-in, understanding, and contribution. After years of experience in a diversity of organizations, a healthy and reliable process of structural change has evolved.

Structural Cybernetics is a high-powered method to build high-performance organizations. It includes a comprehensive implementation handbook (available only to licensees) that documents every aspect of the theory, the products and services of each functional building block, and every step in the implementation process. Structural Cybernetics makes implementing the network organization safe and reliable.

It is our hope that, as students of the science of structural design, a new breed of executives will begin to sort out the management issues that hamper their staff, so that they in turn can bring strategic innovation to people throughout their client communities.

About the Author

N. Dean Meyer -- recognized as one of the foremost authorities on organizational structure -- has made organizational health his life's work. He has been teaching, lecturing, and consulting since 1968, and is known for his systematic approaches to difficult leadership issues.

Meyer founded NDMA Inc. in 1982 to focus exclusively on organizational issues. He is widely published, and coauthor of the book, *The Information Edge,* originally published by McGraw-Hill and now in its sixth printing. His research is documented in two major studies: *Structural Cybernetics,* and *The Internal Economy, A Market Approach.*

Meyer has implemented Structural Cybernetics in dozens of diverse corporate and public-sector organizations.